SHOTS IN THE DARK

THE SNIPER
THE SUBURBS AND THE
THINGS WE VALUE MOST

Shots in the Dark: The Sniper, The Suburbs, and the Things We Value Most

Scripture references are from the King James Version.

Ambassador Emerald International
427 Wade Hampton Boulevard
Greenville, S.C. 29609 U.S.A.

and

Ambassador Productions Ltd.
Providence House
Ardenlee Street
Belfast BT6 8QJ, Northern Ireland

www.emeraldhouse.com

Cover design and page layout by A & E Media, Sam Laterza

ISBN 1 889893 94 3

Shots IN THE Dark

The Sniper
The Suburbs and The Things We Value Most

Mark Ward, Sr.

AMBASSADOR
EMERALD INTERNATIONAL

Greenville, South Carolina • Belfast, Northern Ireland
www.emeraldhouse.com

To my loved ones,
Donna, Laura, and Mark Jr.,
who give me comfort,
And to all the loved ones
who need to be comforted

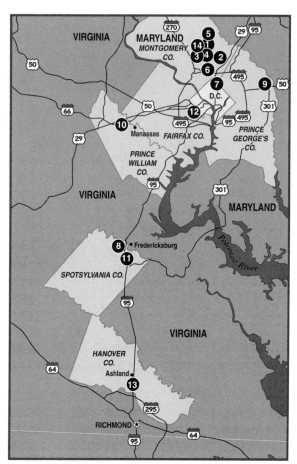

1. Wed, Oct 2, 5:20 PM. Michaels Arts and Crafts, Aspen Hill MD. Window shot, no injuries.

2. Wed, Oct 2, 6:04 PM. Shoppers Food Warehouse, Wheaton MD. James Martin killed.

3. Thu, Oct 3, 7:41 AM. Rockville Pike, White Flint MD. Sonny Buchanan killed.

4. Thu, Oct 3, 8:12 AM. Mobil gas station, Aspen Hill MD. Premkumar Walekar killed.

5. Thu, Oct 3, 8:37 AM. Post office bench, Leisure World MD. Sarah Ramos killed.

6. Thu, Oct 3, 9:58 AM. Shell gas station, Kensington MD. Lore Lewis Rivera killed.

7. Thu, Oct 3, 9:20 PM. Connecticut Avenue NW, Washington DC, Pascal Charlot killed.

8. Fri, Oct 4, 2:30 PM. Michaels Arts and Crafts near I-95, Spotsylvania VA. Unidentified woman wounded.

9. Mon, Oct 7, 8:09 AM. Tasker Middle School near Route 50, Bowie MD. Unidentified student wounded.

10. Wed, Oct 9, 8:18 PM. SSunoco gas station near I-66, Prince William County VA. Dean Meyers killed.

11. Fri, Oct 11, 9:30 AM. Exxon gas station near I-95, Spotsylvania VA. Kenneth Bridges killed.

12. Mon, Oct 14, 9:15 PM. Home Depot, Fairfax VA. Linda Franklin killed.

13. Sat, Oct 19, 7:59 pm. Ponderosa Steakhouse near I-95, Ashland VA. Unidentified man wounded.

14. Tue, Oct 22, 5:56 AM. Parked bus, Aspen Hill MD. Conrad Johnson killed.

Contents

Introduction viii

Dateline: 10.03.02 1

Chapter 1: The Supermarket 5
   and the Things We Value: Abundance

Dateline: 10.04.02 15

Chapter 2: The Shopping Mall 17
   and the Things We Value: Convenience

Dateline: 10.07.02 25

Chapter 3: The Middle School 29
   and the Things We Value: Tolerance

Dateline: 10.09.02 39

Chapter 4: The Gas Station 41
   and the Things We Value: Autonomy

Dateline: 10.11.02 49

Chapter 5: The Interstate 53
   and the Things We Value: Mobility

Dateline: 10.14.02 61

Chapter 6: The Parking Lot 65
   and the Things We Value: Choices

Dateline: 10.19.02 73

Chapter 7: The Restaurant 77
   and the Things We Value: Leisure

Dateline: 10.22.02 91

Chapter 8: The Bus Stop 97
   and the Things We Value: Time

Dateline: 10.24.02 105

Epilogue: The Rest Stop 115
   and the Questions That Remain

Acknowledgments 119

About The Author 121

About You 123

Introduction

In October 2002, America was confronted with a new form of domestic terrorism. Fourteen times in twenty days, an unseen sniper paralyzed the capital of a great nation. We were shocked at the calculated yet indiscriminate violence—a trail of terror that left ten dead, three wounded.

Killing sprees and serial murders are, sadly, not unknown to us. Neither is the daily violence of our cities any less horrifying because it does not make the national news. But we sensed that the attacks of the "D.C. Sniper" were somehow different. "Sometimes it is a historian's sad duty to confess that history is no guide," said Roger Lane, a criminal justice historian. "I can think of no similar shooting or murder pattern in American history."

So we are left to ask, How could it happen? Why was the terror so complete? What does it all mean? Could it happen again?

Seemingly, the sniper turned our contemporary way of life against us. In our cities and suburbs today we enjoy unprecedented mobility. The sniper used that same mobility to suddenly strike at will across an entire region and just as quickly vanish. His targets were not just people but the very things we cannot live without. Shopping centers, gas stations, parking lots, interstate ramps—these are the essence of our lives today. They are things that give us personal freedom, that put us in control.

How could it happen? The sole reason for the sniper killings in Washington, D.C., is the evil of the gunmen. But when we ask why the terror was so great, the answer is not so simple. In a horrible way that no one would have ever wished, the D.C. Sniper held a mirror to our lives. We were uniquely terrified because the killers threatened the things we value most—our safety and our families, but also our unprecedented ability to go where we please today and acquire what we want.

It is not wrong to value a high standard of living. If America can afford prosperity for its people, then we can be grateful. Yet a single sniper's bullet brought a great city of four million people to a standstill.

Despite the unparalleled conveniences and choices that we enjoy today, despite our almost unimaginable degree of personal empowerment, suddenly we are more vulnerable than we ever thought. The things we depend on are more fragile than we knew.

And so the question, What does it mean? All my years I have lived the life of suburbia. I have put up with the long commutes, the fast pace, the job changes. And I have enjoyed the rewards, the expanded career opportunities, the increased options. But if the things I have valued are impermanent, what then? This book is my attempt to struggle with that question and find some answers.

The questions raised by the D.C. Sniper shootings are very personal to me in another way, for the Nation's Capital is my hometown. Washington and its suburbs have been the home of my family for five generations. I was born there in the Fifties, my father a government contractor employed by the U.S. Congress, as were his father and grandfather before him. The events of our time—the Cuban Missile Crisis, the Kennedy and King assassinations, the civil rights marches and antiwar demonstrations, Watergate and Vietnam—had actual personal consequences for my family as I grew up.

In time, I made a career of my own—congressional employee, political reporter, communications executive, broadcaster—and raised a family in Washington. At last when my children were grown, God moved me to a new ministry in another state. Some forty years after my birth in the Nation's Capital, I left a city that was vastly changed from the Washington of my youth. I have seen neighborhood shopping centers turned into mega-malls, farms into freeways, wooded hills into subdivisions.

The places where the D.C. Sniper struck are more than pictures on the evening news to me. I know these places. Two of the shooting sites are only blocks from jobs I once held. Two are gas stations where I have often filled my car, three are at interstate ramps I have frequently used. One is near my boyhood home and two more are just minutes away from where my mother lives today. Yes, I know these places. And I know how these places have changed over the decades, changes that reflect the way we live today—and changes that, for all their benefits, have made these places into targets for a new kind of domestic terror.

The gunmen targeted each place because it stands for something important to us, something we value. In writing this book I was struck how each of the sites stands for a different aspect of our lives in the suburbs today—aspects such as mobility, autonomy, choices, and convenience. These desires are not wrong. Yet anytime we are forced to confront our priorities, even under tragic circumstances, there is an opportunity for self-examination and personal growth.

At the outset, I want to be very clear. In exploring and questioning our values, in no way do I suggest the victims brought tragedy upon themselves. They were only doing the things we all do. Sadly, they were in the wrong place at the wrong time—but certainly *not* for any wrong reasons. Their lives and careers, as you will read in this book, are remembered by all who knew them as assets to their communities.

One of these was Dean Harold Meyers. You will read more about him later. He was given one of the best eulogies a man can receive, "He always remembered everyone's birthday." At his funeral, friends and loved ones asked, Why do bad things happen to good people? As Meyers' pastor put it, "Why did someone so full of life have to die?" It is a question asked by all those who were touched by the ten tragic deaths of October 2002.

I would not try to answer that question, for I have never lost a loved one to a senseless murder. But consider the words of someone who has. Reflecting on his brother's death, Bob Meyers said that he grieved deeply, "but a long time ago we chose to trust God rather than question Him. There was two inches between my brother being hit and not being hit. Who am I to question something like this?" Bob Meyers believed that "you've got to decide for yourself whether you're going to be bitter or angry against God, or you're going to believe that God is big enough and strong enough and powerful enough that He knows what's going on." It was a decision, Meyers said, he had already made two years earlier. When his wife of twenty-seven years died in a car accident, he struggled with feelings of anger and bitterness. But instead, Bob Meyers decided to trust God.

That is the real issue, whether to trust God. There is nothing wrong with enjoying the personal freedom and prosperity our modern way of life can afford. But now we know, in the aftermath of the D.C. Sniper, that the things we value—mobility, autonomy, choices, convenience—can be fragile, vulnerable, impermanent. God offers us values that are both practical for the way we live today and yet are lasting and cannot be taken away. Will we trust Him?

10.03.02

Montgomery County, Md. — Five people going about the prosaic chores of daily life were indiscriminately shot dead in a 17-hour span in Montgomery County ... Police said they believe that all were slain by an elusive assailant, acting alone or with an accomplice, who prowled the normally peaceful sidewalks and shopping centers of suburbia, squeezing off shots and then vanishing unnoticed. The killings — all single-shot, sniper-like attacks, police said — occurred outdoors in public places ...*

On October 2, 2002, at 5:20 p.m., a single bullet pierced the plate-glass window of the Michaels Arts and Crafts store at 13850 Georgia Avenue in Aspen Hill, Maryland. The shot narrowly missed a cashier inside. It would be the last time that the D.C. Sniper would miss.

A stray bullet in a store window is not news in the Nation's Capital. The incident did not even make it into the papers the next day. But forty-four minutes after that first errant shot, the gunman did not miss a second time. Within seventeen hours, five suburbanites were dead and the story was front-page news across the country.

About 6 p.m. on October 2, James D. Martin, 55, emerged from the Shoppers Food Warehouse at 2201 Randolph Road in Wheaton, Maryland. He had purchased sodas and snacks for his son's church youth group and was taking the items to his car. The shopping center on Randolph Road is a popular destination, located on a busy avenue near the confluence five major suburban commuter routes. So the parking lot was crowded with Wednesday evening shoppers on the way home from work.

At 6:04 p.m., Martin was struck by a single gunshot from a high-powered rifle. Montgomery County police officers, posted

*News bulletins in this book are excerpted from the actual *Washington Post* accounts.

1

across the street at the Glenmont station, heard the shot and rushed to the scene. A crowd of shoppers had gathered in the parking lot, attempting to administer CPR but unable to save the victim. No one witnessed the shooting, which apparently was made from a distance by an unseen sniper.

The following morning at 7:41 a.m., October 3, a third sniper shooting occurred a few miles west of Randolph Road. James L. "Sonny" Buchanan Jr., 39, was pushing a lawn mower on the 11000 block of Rockville Pike near the White Flint Auto Mall, when a single shot struck him fatally in the chest. He had recently gotten out of the landscaping business and moved to Virginia, but was trimming the grass for an old customer who needed a favor.

Thirty-one minutes later, at 8:12 a.m., another shot rang out in the nearby suburb of Aspen Hill. A cab driver, Premkumar A. Walekar, 54, had just bought some lottery tickets at the Mobil gas station on Connecticut Avenue, one of the busiest commuter routes in Montgomery County. He was shot and killed as he stood beside his cab. An Indian immigrant who had lived in the United States for thirty-six years, Walekar's eldest daughter was about to graduate from college.

The sniper proceeded north on Connecticut Avenue and Georgia Avenue, then onto Rossmoor Boulevard and past the large Leisure World retirement community. At 8:37 a.m., twenty-five minutes after the last shooting, another victim was gunned down, shot in the head. Sarah Ramos, 34, was seated on a bench at the post office on 3701 Rossmoor Boulevard, adjacent to the Leisure World complex. A housekeeper and babysitter, she was waiting for an employer to pick her up. Ramos left behind a husband and seven-year-old son.

By 9:58 a.m. the morning rush hour had subsided and Lori Lewis Rivera, 25, a mother from Silver Spring, was vacuuming her minivan at the Shell station on Connecticut Avenue and Knowles Road in Kensington. For the fifth time in a seventeen-hour span, a single shot was fired and a random victim was dead. Rivera was married and had a young daughter.

Throughout the day, police worked to find any clues or witnesses. Few leads turned up. Most promising was a report from the Leisure World shooting. A man who worked at the complex as a landscaper or cleaner had seen a white box truck leaving the scene. The man spoke only Spanish and was interviewed by a Montgomery County policemen stationed at the Wheaton precinct a mile away.

Despite the lack of clues, the elusive gunmen seemed to be following a geographic pattern. That pattern apparently continued when the next killing occurred one block south of the Montgomery County line in the District of Columbia, 9:20 p.m., October 3. Pascal Charlot, 72, was shot in the neck as he stood at the corner of Kalmia Road and Connecticut Avenue N.W.

A carpenter by trade, Charlot immigrated from Haiti to the United States in 1964 and earned his living as a home remodeler, raising five children. An hour before the slaying he had cooked supper for his wife, an Alzheimer's sufferer, then left the couple's red brick rowhouse to run an errand. After the attack some witnesses reported seeing a boxy-looking "burgundy" car driving with its lights off; one witness identified it as a Chevy Caprice. But police, who were quickly being overwhelmed with tips, discounted any importance to the sighting.

Two days, seven shots, six dead. Yet, horrific as the cold-blooded killings were, they seemed confined to a restricted area. Police surmised they were dealing with a murder spree that resembled the "classic" pattern of other serial killings, where the murderer targets a geographic area or certain type of victim. Washington was horrified but, on Day 2 of the shootings, it was the residents of Montgomery County who mostly seemed affected. All the killings had occurred within about a two-and-a-half-mile radius. There was fear along Connecticut Avenue, but the Nation's Capital was not yet in terror.

Chapter One

The Supermarket
and the Things We Value: Abundance

Going shopping. Getting gas. Going to work, to school, out to eat. For most Americans, these are the things of our everyday lives. In October 2002 when a sniper launched a reign of terror, his targets were not just people. The horrific shootings attacked the very basis of our lives today, the things we take for granted.

And so for twenty terrifying days the people of Washington, D.C., my hometown, were transfixed by the awful news. Soon the whole nation was also watching in stunned disbelief. This was not about airliners crashing into skyscrapers. This was parking lots and shopping centers, middle schools and gas stations, bus stops and freeway exits, Home Depot and the Ponderosa Steakhouse. This was mothers keeping their kids at home, commuters afraid to fill their tanks, high school football games being canceled. This was our way of life.

The Maryland suburbs of Wheaton and White Oak, Rockville and Aspen Hill, are well known to me. Just a few years ago when I worked at a local Christian radio station, I would often visit the many African-American churches in the Maryland suburbs—vibrant congregations with names such as New Covenant Church, Victory Christian Ministries, Full Gospel Baptist Church, Shield of Faith Christian Center, and Greater Lighthouse Church.

That was the best part of radio work, leaving the isolation of the studio and visiting churches and listeners around the Washington area. I always liked the suburbs of Montgomery County, pleasant neighborhoods with trees and green lawns, a mix of old houses and new. As *The Washington Post* put it, the "peaceful sidewalks and shopping centers of suburbia." This could have been my own suburb, it looked much the same. When I passed the Shoppers Food Warehouse on Randolph Road in Wheaton, it was the very image of the one my wife and I used each week in Virginia.

When I heard that James Martin had been shot by a sniper in the parking lot of that same Shoppers Food Warehouse on Randolph Road, I felt instinctively that it could have been me. He was just a dad buying some snacks for his son's church youth group, then trying to beat the rush hour traffic home on a Friday night. How many times had I done the same?

Plenty of Everything

In the Washington of my boyhood there were no Shoppers Food Warehouses. Randolph Road was a neighborhood street, and the future site of my Virginia store was a farm in the countryside. We had supermarkets in those days, but they were locally owned. The Wal-Mart Revolution of "big box" chain stores was far in the future. We had few packaged snacks or, really, pre-cooked foods of any kind. Getting some goodies for the youth group would have meant baking cookies from scratch and mixing up some punch or juice.

Today, of course, mom or dad can just pick up some snacks and soda at Shoppers Food Warehouse. The choices are quick, convenient, cheap, and abundant. Mom can relax, and dad can just pop into the store on the way home from work. What could be easier–especially when we can rely on our suburban superstore to have everything we could possibly want, and at a good price?

The way things work has always fascinated me. So as a writer I enjoy doing articles for business journals. The work is interesting and I often get a behind-the-scenes look at things that we usually take for granted. When I had the chance to interview a top executive with a leading superstore chain, I was amazed at how profoundly the business has been transformed.

A decade ago her company operated a chain of conventional supermarkets. Since then, the chain has upgraded its locations to feature fresh bakeries, pharmacies, florists, automotive and houseware departments, paperback books and greeting cards, photo processing, video rentals, automatic teller machines, and bar-code scanning. All units have been converted to 24/7 operation. New stores are built with a hundred thousand square feet of space and provide supervised play areas for children, in-store banking with flexible hours, laundry and dry cleaning service, and gas pumps in the parking lot.

What ties it all together? The executive told me her company was committed to "providing people with the various things they need to make their life taste just a little bit better—and that goes beyond food. We want our customers to taste more of everything that's important to them. For example, our pricing policies help people save more for other things they need. Video rentals create opportunities for family nights at home. And our fueling facilities, just like our pharmacies and our dry cleaners, mean that customers can run one less errand."

A Different Worry

That is a good summary of suburban living today, for people "to taste more of everything that's important to them." And there is nothing wrong with that. If America is a land of plenty, if we have enjoyed economic good times, then we have reason to be glad. Yet many who live in suburbia today, especially younger families, have never known anything but plenty. Eating out, buying the latest electronic gear, easy credit—this is the way we live today.

The Washington in which I grew up had a different outlook. I did not live, as my parents did, during the Depression and the war. But as a child living in Washington, I did have one worry that we lived with every day.

I was four years old when—exactly forty years before the D.C. Sniper—my hometown faced an even greater threat. It was October 1962. Soviet missiles had been discovered on the island of Cuba. Communist revolutionaries had taken power there just three years earlier. The missiles, once operational, could reach Washington— could reach my house—in ten minutes. I remember my father and mother packing our suitcases and mapping a route to West Virginia. Today, recently unclassified documents show that nuclear war was even closer than we knew. The unthinkable was averted, yet the Washington that I knew was never the same. Other people in other places could go back to their daily business. We were Ground Zero.

Every day when I walked to my elementary school in Arlington, at the top of the hill was a telephone pole at the corner of Manchester Street and Eighth Road. On top of the pole was a box with a trumpet attached. Once a month they would test it. Anyone who has ever heard an air raid siren will never forget it; I have not. Over the door of my school was a yellow-and-black sign indicating a nuclear fallout shelter. This was part of everyday life in the Washington of my youth. We did not talk about it, but we all knew it was there.

Much later, the air raid sirens and black-and-yellow signs were taken down. In the Nineties when I worked at the radio station, even the Emergency Broadcast System ("This is only a test. If this

7

were an actual emergency ...") was dismantled. But in the Washington where I grew up, good times were hard to take for granted. From my hometown, the world did not seem like a place where anything was guaranteed.

Want To Be a Millionaire?

The house next door to mine was often rented by military families. Washington is like that, as people in government service rotate in and out every two or three years. Some of our neighbors worked at the Pentagon after doing tours of duty in Vietnam. My parents watched the news anxiously and, to their relief, the war ended less than a year before my eighteenth birthday. Other parents in our neighborhood were not so fortunate.

In the years that followed, however, as a young adult living in Washington I was greatly affected by a legacy of that war—inflation. At one point, the cost of living was rising nearly twenty percent a year. Annual raises of ten percent or more were standard. The joke that made the rounds of Washington in those days was, "Soon we'll all be millionaires! We'll even be able to buy a fifty-thousand-dollar hamburger!"

How high was inflation? When Donna and I were married we had to act as quickly as possible to find a down payment and buy a house. Somehow we did it, and felt lucky to get an interest rate of only fourteen percent. But we had to buy while we could still afford it. The longer we waited, the less likely we could ever own a home of our own. By the time inflation was tamed, we were glad to "only" be in a recession.

Terms of Service

Or was it a recession? Ronald Reagan put it well. "A recession is when other people lose *their* jobs," he said, "and a depression is when you lose *your* job." When I learned that lesson the hard way, I also learned about another aspect of life in Washington.

My father had changed careers by then and moved to the Midwest. When I would come to visit, neighbors who met me would say, "Oh, you're Pete and Carolyn's son?" They identified me by family. In Washington every introduction includes the question, "What do you do?" Answering that simple yet unavoidable question was one of the hardest aspects of being "between jobs."

So I did all the right things. I sent out resumes by the score. And then God did a work in my life.

As a native Washingtonian I love my city. Its way of life seems normal and natural to me. I also wanted to serve God—but only if I could live where I wanted and have the job title and salary I wanted. I was willing to serve Him, but only on *my* terms. In the suburbs I had grown up to expect certain things out of life. God had to take it all away before He could use me. After a year of failed job interviews and rejection letters, I at last came to God and prayed, "Use me, Lord. Whatever, whenever, wherever. You tell me and I will do it!" Only when I was completely broken, when my only desire was to serve God on *His* terms, could His plan for my life unfold.

A few days later I saw a white 3x5 index card on the bulletin board of my church in suburban Springfield. A Christian ministry was in need of a—communications manager! I couldn't believe it. That was exactly what I had been doing in my years since college.

God put me to the test. I had to leave Washington and live in the rural North. I had to take a fifty percent salary cut. And the week after I accepted the job, a major Washington organization offered me an executive position with a significant pay raise. But I turned it down without hesitation. Having seen the way God was working in my life, I was not about to miss out on the excitement!

My greatest victories, my greatest spiritual breakthroughs, have often come after my greatest trials. Though I firmly hope that the abundance and prosperity our nation enjoys today will continue, I still wonder: Can a people who are filled ever experience the power of God?

The Open Door

The people who lived in my Washington neighborhoods are probably like the people in your city. They are good people who work hard and try to do right. So if you ask a neighbor or co-worker to accept Christ, why do they say no? The frequent answer is, "I just don't see a need for it."

How do you answer that objection? What can the Bible say to the people in your suburb, your neighbors who have good jobs and nice houses, who drive three cars and take two annual vacations? To people who, frankly, live better than you?

Jesus said, "I am come that they might have life, and that they might have it more abundantly" (John 10:10). It's a familiar verse we often quote. But what does it really mean? What is an "abundant life"? At Shoppers Food Warehouse we can see and smell and touch (and buy) the abundance arrayed before us. It is tangible. So what is Jesus talking about? To find the answer, let us look at the entire passage.

> *Then said Jesus unto them again, Verily, verily, I say unto you, I am the door of the sheep. All that ever came before me are thieves and robbers: but the sheep did not hear them. I am the door: by me if any man enter in, he shall be saved, and shall go in and out, and find pasture. The thief cometh not, but for to steal, and to kill, and to destroy: I am come that they might have life, and that they might have it more abundantly. I am the good shepherd: the good shepherd giveth his life for the sheep. (John 10:7-11)*

Imagine a flock of sheep. These sheep are kept in a pen and belong to a certain shepherd who loves and cares for them. The sheep pen has a door that opens into an abundant pasture where the flock can graze and be fed. Jesus is that door, and He beckons to all that "if any man hear my voice, and open the door, I will come in to him, and will sup with him, and he with me" (Revelation 3:20).

Only one door leads to the abundance of the pasture. When a thief enters the pen, he gestures toward the wrong door. The sheep who have no shepherd are in danger. They do not know the shepherd's voice and so heed the call to enter the wrong door, the door to destruction. But the sheep that belong to the shepherd won't listen. They follow only the voice of Jesus, the good shepherd. So they enter confidently at the door which leads to abundance, even though "strait is the gate, and narrow is the way, which leadeth unto life" (Matthew 7:14).

That the issue is either salvation or damnation is put plainly in Luke 13:23-27, "Then said one unto him, Lord, are there few that be saved? And he said unto them, Strive to enter in at the strait gate: for many, I say unto you, will seek to enter in, and shall not be able. When once the master of the house is risen up, and hath shut the door, and ye begin to stand without, and to knock at the door, saying, Lord, Lord, open unto us; and he shall answer and say unto you, I know you not [who] ye are ... depart from me, all ye workers of iniquity."

While a man yet lives the door remains open, the choice still available. But when the span of life is over, then "it is appointed unto men once to die, but after this the judgment" (Hebrews 9:27). At last the Master shuts the door. All who are on the outside will knock, "Let me in! Let me in!" But the Master will reply, "I don't know you! Go away!"

An Unbeatable Offer

Those who put their trust in Christ have an open door to the most abundant pasture of all, to the very storehouses of the God who "shall supply all your need according to his riches in glory by Christ Jesus" (Philippians 4:19). And did you notice that, in declaring He had come so that we "might have [life] more abundantly," Jesus also said He "giveth his life for the sheep"? There is a connection between the two, and it becomes clear when we learn, "For ye know the grace of our Lord Jesus Christ, that, though he was rich, yet for your sakes he became poor, that ye through his poverty might be rich" (2 Corinthians 8:9).

I do not believe in making deals with God. Simply stated, the Lord promises to the believer that 1) He knows all your needs, so that 2) all you have to do is follow Him, and then 3) He will supply your needs and 4) you do not have to worry about it! Here is the contract God offers you and me:

> Therefore I say unto you, Take no thought for your life, what ye shall eat, or what ye shall drink; nor yet for your body, what ye shall put on. Is not the life more than meat, and the body than raiment? Behold the fowls of the air: for they sow not, neither do they reap, nor gather into barns; yet your heavenly Father feedeth them. Are ye not much better than they? Which of you by taking thought [i.e., worrying] can add one cubit unto his stature? And why take ye thought for raiment? Consider the lilies of the field, how they grow; they toil not, neither do they spin: And yet I say unto you, That even Solomon in all his glory was not arrayed like one of these. Wherefore, if God so clothe the grass of the field, which to day is, and to morrow is cast into the oven, shall he not much more clothe you, O ye of little faith? Therefore take no thought, saying, What shall we eat? or, What shall we drink? or, Wherewithal shall we be clothed? (For after all these things do the Gentiles seek:) for your heavenly Father knoweth that ye have need of all these things. But seek ye first the kingdom of God, and his right-eousness; and all these things shall be added unto you. Take therefore no thought for the morrow: for the morrow shall take thought for the things of itself. Sufficient unto the day is the evil thereof (Matthew 6:25-34).

The man who follows God in the confident knowledge that He will supply all his needs can say, "I have learned, in whatsoever state I am, therewith to be content. I know both how to be abased, and I know how to abound ... I can do all things through Christ which

11

strengtheneth me" (Philippians 4:11-13). That man can testify, "But godliness with contentment is great gain. For we brought nothing into this world, and it is certain we can carry nothing out. And having food and raiment let us be therewith content" (1 Timothy 6:6-8).

Give and Take

After I surrendered my will to serve God on *His* terms rather than my own, that dedication has often been put to the test. One of those tests concerns a favorite topic of conversation in Washington—in this case, not politics or the Redskins but real estate.

When Donna and I were married we bought a condo. Six months later we sold it for enough profit to put down on a house in a nice suburban neighborhood. Seven years later when God called us to the ministry, we relocated to another state and sold our D.C. house for nearly double its original price. Then after five more years, when God called us back to Washington and another ministry, we had to sell when the market was in a slump. Forced to take less for our house than we paid, much of our equity was lost. In another five years as God called me to relocate to my present ministry, again we lost money.

According to my suburban values, it was not supposed to happen this way. I asked myself, "What is it worth to me to follow God's will for my life? Is it worth losing all my home equity?" But the answer was clear. "God is in control of the economy, and He doesn't make mistakes. I did not have to do any labor to make my profits in real estate. God gave it to me—and He can take it away."

I had come to the same conclusion as Job. "Naked came I out of my mother's womb, and naked shall I return thither: the Lord gave, and the Lord hath taken away; blessed be the name of the Lord" (Job 1:21). And you know what? God *did* know my need! In moving to my present place of ministry, with our children in college God gave my wife and me a perfect "empty nest" house. I live within walking distance of my work, a commute I can definitely learn to live with! Our house is small, but it meets our needs and is paid for. And now we have more equity than ever before!

Real Abundance

For so many years I chased the suburban dream—a nice home in an attractive neighborhood for my family, and a career that would bring me ever increasing opportunities. To realize my dream I endured the twice-daily commutes on the Beltway, the backups on

Wilson Bridge, the ebb and flow of office politics, the victories and disappointments.

In themselves, there is nothing wrong with these things. Millions of us do them every day, working hard and faithfully for our families and employers. But for me, when I did these for myself so that I might accumulate abundance for my own pleasure, I discovered:

> *Ye have sown much, and bring in little; ye eat, but ye have not enough; ye drink, but ye are not filled with drink; ye clothe you, but there is none warm; and he that earneth wages earneth wages to put it into a bag with holes. (Haggai 1:6)*

How much greater abundance is given to Christians who will "provide yourselves bags which wax not old, a treasure in the heavens that faileth not" (Luke 12:32). For to us is offered the chance to "lay not up for yourselves treasures upon earth ... but lay up for yourselves treasures in heaven, where neither moth nor rust doth corrupt, and where thieves do not break through nor steal" (Matthew 6:19-20).

My youth in Washington was lived under the cloud of political and global unrest. So I am glad that today my hometown, my nation, have grown prosperous and known abundance. And I am saddened, as are we all, by the foreign and domestic terrorism that now haunts our streets—and our thoughts.

We have enjoyed a respite, a period of good times. But in the end, "man is born unto trouble, as the sparks fly upward" (Job 5:7). Good times do not last forever, earthly abundance will someday fail. With a single shot from a sniper's rifle, we discovered that the things we depend on are more fragile than we ever believed. What will we do now? What will *you* do? Perhaps as I did, you might consider the claims of the One who said,

> *I am come that they might have life, and that they might have it more abundantly.*

10.04.02

Spotsylvania County, Va. — The bullet that seriously wounded a Spotsylvania County mother of two while she was loading packages into her minivan outside a mall Friday was fired from the same gun used to kill at least four of the six victims in the series of sniper shootings in Montgomery County and the District, authorities said last night. "The forensic evidence has shown us that their shooting is linked to the Montgomery County shootings, linked to the D.C. shooting," said Montgomery Police Chief Charles A. Moose ...

A t 2:30 p.m., Friday, October 4, a woman had just opened the rear hatch of her minivan and was loading packages into the vehicle. She stood with her back to the road in the parking lot of the Michaels Arts and Craft store, a freestanding building near the massive Spotsylvania Mall. Traffic sped by on Route 3, headed either to the I-95 exit some fourteen hundred feet away or to Route 1 on the other side of the interstate.

Then a sniper's bullet struck the forty-three-year-old woman in the back. She survived. But once the news was flashed by the local media, the entire Washington metro area was instantly convulsed by fear. Until now, the six previous shootings had been confined to less than a three-mile radius in Montgomery County, Maryland. The news from Spotsylvania County changed everything, for the attack was some sixty miles away near Fredericksburg, Virginia, on the extreme southern edge of the metro Washington region.

Fear now mounted to a new level in the Nation's Capital. The Virginia shooting was just off Interstate 95, virtually the main street of the entire Washington metro area, a road that millions of commuters and shoppers use each day. Just as ominous, I-95 and the Washington Beltway provide quick access to and from every jurisdiction in the region. If a killer were roaming the suburban streets of Montgomery County, that would be frightening enough. But if a gunman were now ranging across I-95, even as far as Fredericksburg, that would be truly terrifying. The sniper could strike anywhere.

Ballistics evidence soon linked the Virginia attack to the six slayings in Maryland. In each case, except where bullet fragments were too badly damaged for analysis, forensic examination showed the victims had been shot with the same .223-caliber rifle. Like most rifles, the weapon left distinctive markings on the bullets as they passed through the barrel. With this evidence in hand, police were also investigating a possible connection to a September 14 liquor store robbery in Montgomery County in which a man was wounded.

With the Spotsylvania shooting, the sniper now changed his modus operandi. The Maryland shootings occurred at densely urbanized, close-in suburbs where the killer could use local traffic to mask his escape. For the Virginia attack, the gunman chose a site with easy access to an interstate highway. Some experts also speculated that the gunman might have some connection to Michaels Arts and Crafts, having twice targeted such stores.

Sadly, Spotsylvania County was no stranger to high-profile serial murder cases. In 1996 the brutal killings of three adolescent girls, sisters Katie and Kristin Lisk and neighbor Sofia Silva, made national headlines. Ironically, the case remained unsolved until June 2002 when the killer, who was also suspected in the rape of a South Carolina girl, committed suicide in Florida as police closed in. After six years of concern over a killer on the loose, many Spotsylvania residents were only just getting over their fear. Then the D.C. sniper struck their county.

State Senator John Chichester acknowledged that the 1996 murders and the D.C. Sniper attacks "connects us with the new urbanization of the area ... No more small, sleepy town. That kind of drove it home."

As one resident told *The Washington Post*, "How long can we live with this fear that's controlling us? How long can we stay inside? ... When do we get back to normal? When do we go back to our lives like we used to? Can we ever?"

Chapter Two

The Shopping Mall
and the Things We Value: Convenience

Now and then the Washington papers, the *Post* and *Times* and suburban *Journals*, run articles about the creeping blight of suburban sprawl. Usually the articles are accompanied by photos that show a forest of retail store signs, receding far into the horizon as they line some benighted suburban thoroughfare.

Route 1 in Virginia is such a road. Once, before Interstate 95, it was the main north-south highway of the East Coast that stretched from Maine to Key West. It still does. But in cities like Washington, Route 1 has long since been taken over by storefronts and strip shopping centers. The section I know best starts near the Pentagon and Reagan National Airport, runs past historic Old Town Alexandria, then heads south through Fairfax County neighborhoods like Belle Haven and Hybla Valley, Groveton and Woodbridge.

Passing through Dale City and Dumfries, then Quantico and Aquia, the march of strip stores finally peters out around Fredericksburg. All told, nearly fifty solid miles of fastfood restaurants and gas stations, laundromats and florists, tailors and tanning salons. And then there is the Michaels Arts and Crafts store, the one near Spotsylvania Mall on Route 3 at the nexus of I-95 and Route 1. The one where my mother shops. The one where, on October 4, 2002, at 2:30 p.m., a forty-three-year-old woman (identity withheld) was shot in the back by a sniper's bullet while she loaded purchases into the hatch of her minivan. Thankfully, she survived.

Bypassing the Brands

You know Route 1. You know it well. There are roads just like it in your city too. When in lived in Fairfax County there was a Route 1 Corridor Task Force charged with cleaning up and beautifying the area. Your city probably has such a task force too.

Then again, your city also has a zoning board that keeps issuing permits for more stores. Why? Ordinary people want them, people who vote with their feet and their dollars. Through two homes and twelve years, my wife and I lived just off Route 1. And if the stoplights every two blocks were annoying, the convenience of having every imaginable kind of store within easy driving distance was indispensable.

In the days when my parents shopped in the Washington suburbs, shoppers made their choices based on brand preferences. My dad liked Esso gasoline and was willing to go a little out of his way to use an Esso station. For her part, my mother went to the Grand Union supermarket because they had a good meat section, while other moms might have stuck with Safeway. Sears was our usual choice for school clothes because, well, it's where we always went. It was a solid brand that gave good value. When I was in high school, mom even got her first dishwasher there.

Of course, shopping has changed today. Want gas? Stop at whichever one you happen to be driving by. Fastfood? Whatever is close. Clothing? Check out the sales at all the nearby stores. Survey after survey shows that convenience leads the list of reasons why shoppers make the choices they do. Convenience has, literally, become an industry in itself.

Word Associations

As a writer I enjoy doing many different things. One of those is writing for business journals. Over the years I have written for publications ranging from *Asbestos Abatement* to *Aftermarket Business*, *Rural Builder* to *Recycling Today*, and *Floral Management* to *Fire Journal*. But the work is fascinating. I have interviewed an Olympic gold medalist and a Miss America, a board game inventor and a teenage millionaire, the presidents of Domino's Pizza and Federal Express.

Washington is a wonderful place to be a writer. Not only is it the news capital of the world. After the government, one of the city's leading employers are organizations that *lobby* the government. These include political advocacy groups, think tanks, nonprofits, and an astonishing array of industry, trade, and professional associations. There is even an association for people who work for associations—the American Society of Association Executives. Altogether, more than twenty thousand national organizations make their headquarters in the Washington area—and most of them publish magazines.

I have written for the magazines of the National Association of Truck Stop Operators, the International Automobile Dealers Association, the Society of Independent Gasoline Marketers of America, the American School Food Service Association, the National School Boards Association—to name a few. Yes, Washington is a great city. Where else could the American Public Health Association and the Snack Food Association be neighbors!

So it is not surprising that I have written about convenience—why consumers crave it, how businesses provide it. It is the key to understanding why Route 1 keeps right on sprouting more storefronts, and why a sniper's bullet at a Michaels Arts and Crafts in Fredericksburg terrorized a region of more than four million people.

Drive-Thru Example

Convenience? Consider what it takes to bring you a drive-thru hamburger. When I wrote this article for a retail journal I was amazed at the great lengths to which retailers go, just to ensure that you always get what they want, when you want it.

Drive-thrus are no "field of dreams." Simply building a unit doesn't ensure a steady stream of customers. You have to do it right, retailers say, because it's very easy to do it wrong ...

"You need at least $50,000 to build even a decent drive-thru," one designer estimates, "and that's the bare minimum for the cash register, window, lighting, canopy, landscaping, ice and coffee holders, and all the rest. Then on top of that, you've got your labor and operating costs."

To keep its customers happy, one fastfood operator installed not only a new drive-thru lane but also fanciful water fountains activated by motion sensors. "Giving your customers some entertainment—and managing their perception of waiting time—is critically important to providing them a positive experience so they'll want to come back."

Another critical factor, he suggests, is having the managerial savvy to keep drive-thru orders moving quickly. Every single drive-thru sale is clocked. Computers then keep tabs on transaction times with daily, weekly, and monthly reports. With these tools, the company has kept transaction times to an average of 1 minute, 40 seconds ...

My article went on to describe industry standards for the drive-thru lane (clearly marked with signs, at least twelve feet wide and five feet from the building, long enough for at least five cars, no more than one lefthand turn, and a wide enough radius to accommodate minivans and pickups), and the pickup window "should project out from the building to provide customers a more comfortable reach and let them see employees working on their orders."

In another business journal article, the president of a leading convenience store chain explained to me how his locations were "as well thought out as a grandmaster chess game." The outside of each store features a bright color scheme that can not be missed. Lighting is actually more powerful than sunlight, with the reflection intensified by the white concrete paving of the parking area. Gas pumps are placed for maximum visual effect from the street. Inside the store, even cash registers beep with the sounds of video games to create an exciting atmosphere.

Likewise, the CEO of another national chain agreed that convenience is critical because "customer perception of any quality difference among [brands] is diminishing. Baby Boomers and Generation Xers didn't grow up with the brand names that are around today, and all the recent mega-mergers are further dissipating brand identities ... We just have to make sure the stores we [operate] are more attractive and offer better service" than the competition.

Convenient Christianity?

Convenience is good business. But is it good Christianity? Do not get me wrong. I do not think that Christians must take monastic vows, sleep on cold floors, and make a virtue out of being inconvenienced. If suburban life can offer modern conveniences— accessible stores, drive-thru hamburgers, automatic teller machines, even online shopping—I am glad.

But then I get angry when the woman in front of me at the checkout line decides to write a check. I grumble when my car gets stuck behind a "left lane bandit." I murmur when the best parking spaces at the mall (or at church) are already taken. I fume when a web page takes fifteen seconds to load. *I'm being inconvenienced! Don't they know it's me!*

Of course, neither did my dad like it when the Esso station closed five minutes before he got there. And my mother was not exactly thrilled when the lady in front of her at the Grand Union needed a price check. But in a world where we can pay at the pump, where grocery items are bar-coded and scanned, we are no longer grateful for conveniences. We expect them.

When I started my career as a Washington writer and editor I was thrilled to have an electric typewriter and a bottle of White-Out. At deadline, I delivered my galleys to the printer via first-class mail. Fax machines and overnight delivery were not common until the Nineties. Yet today I even get impatient with people who do not check their e-mail every day.

If we are honest, then we will admit it. When we are inconvenienced we feel like we have been violated, taken advantage of. The carefully woven web of our suburban lives unravels and our psyches cannot cope. We break down; we are vulnerable. And so a single shot from a sniper, in a strip store parking lot in Spotsylvania County, leaves the capital of the world's greatest nation in terror.

The Right Kind of Neighborhood

I am as guilty of rebelling at inconvenience as the next guy. So I have had to search the scriptures to find the right response, the right outlook—and then constantly remind myself to apply God's Word in my daily situations.

The first principle I discovered is that a Christian *should* be concerned about convenience—the convenience of *others*. "Look not every man on his own things, but every man also on the things of others" (Philippians 2:4).

Most Sunday school children know Jesus' admonition, "And unto him that smiteth thee on the one cheek offer also the other; and him that taketh away thy cloak forbid not to take thy coat also" (Luke 6:29). Yet turning the other cheek is not just an action, it is an ethic. "For though I be free from all men, yet have I made myself servant unto all, that I might gain the more" converts to Christ (1 Corinthians 9:19).

One of the most familiar passages of the New Testament is Paul's plea in Romans 12:1, "I beseech you therefore, brethren, by the mercies of God, that ye present your bodies a living sacrifice, holy, acceptable unto God, which is your reasonable service." In the next verse the apostle explains that we become acceptable to God by being "not conformed to this world" but instead "transformed by the renewing of your mind, that ye may prove what is that good, and acceptable, and perfect, will of God" (12:2).

And what then is the perfect will of God? The next verse puts its succinctly. "For I say, through the grace given unto me, to every man that is among you, not to think of himself more highly than he ought to think; but to think soberly, according as God hath dealt to every man the measure of faith" (12:3). Putting others before self is manifested as each Christian does his part, exercising the gifts God has given him, for the corporate good (12:4-9). But then read what happens as people seek not their own convenience but the convenience of others.

> *Be kindly affectioned one to another with brotherly love; in honour preferring one another; not slothful in business; fervent in spirit; serving the Lord; rejoicing in hope; patient in tribulation; continuing instant in prayer; distributing to the necessity of saints; given to hospitality. Bless them which persecute you: bless, and curse not. Rejoice with them that do rejoice, and weep with them that weep. Be of the same mind one toward another. Mind not high things, but condescend to men of low estate. Be not wise in your own conceits. Recompense to no man evil for evil. Provide things honest in the sight of all men. If it be possible, as much as lieth in you, live peaceably with all men ... Therefore if thine enemy hunger, feed him; if he thirst, give him drink ... Be not overcome of evil, but overcome evil with good. (Romans 12:10-21)*

That sounds like the kind of suburb I would like to live in! A neighborhood where people are kind, hard-working, patient, charitable, hospitable, sympathetic, honest. We live in a society where the conveniences we enjoy exist because we demand them—or we will take our business elsewhere! God wants us to live in a world where we enjoy conveniences because everyone is committed to serving everyone else.

Jesus said, "If any man desire to be first, the same shall be last of all, and servant of all" (Mark 9:35). And He set the ultimate example. "Even as the Son of man came not to be ministered unto, but to minister, and to give his life a ransom for many" (Matthew 20:28).

A Blessed Irony

The second principle I learned from God's Word is that as Christians we have no rights. I am nothing and I deserve nothing. All I have, all I am, all I will ever be, I owe to God. "For whether we live, we live unto the Lord; and whether we die, we die unto the Lord: whether we live therefore, or die, we are the Lord's" (Romans 14:8).

Indeed, far from ease and convenience, the Christian is promised only trial and trouble in this life. "Yea, and all that will live godly in Christ Jesus shall suffer persecution" (2 Timothy 3:12). Jesus Himself declared, "Behold, I send you forth as sheep in the midst of wolves ... And ye shall be hated of all men for my name's sake: but he that endureth to the end shall be saved" (Matthew 10:16, 22).

But the blessed irony is that by dying to self the Christian gains everything (Philippians 1:21), for "thou art no more a servant, but a son; and if a son, then an heir of God through Christ" (Galatians 4:7).

How do you "die to self"? Take a vow of poverty, perhaps? Promise God you will start being a good person? No, you do it by admitting you *can not* do good on your own. Then repent and throw yourself on the mercy of Christ, accept the gift of His payment for your sins, and trust Him as the Savior you need. And that is when you can say,

I am crucified with Christ: neverthless I live; yet not I, but Christ liveth in me" (Galatians 2:20).

10.07.02

Prince George's County, Md. — A 13-year-old boy was critically wounded outside a Prince George's County school [Monday] in a shooting that authorities linked to a spate of sniper attacks that have now killed six people and wounded two others in the Washington area since Wednesday. The youth, an eighth-grader at Benjamin Tasker Middle School in Bowie, was struck in the chest by a high-powered rifle bullet as he was being dropped off in front of the school by an aunt about 8 a.m. ...

Most students at Benjamin Tasker Middle School ride the bus. With four major roads and two cloverleaf interchanges in a two-mile radius, walking to school is not practical. Less than nine hundred feet away is the entrance ramp to Route 50, an interstate-grade highway that links Washington with the Maryland state capitol at Annapolis. About two miles east is Route 301, the major roadway for southern Maryland.

Tasker Middle School is right at the hub of these two highways. The campus is also fronted on the west by Collington Road, a major suburban avenue. But to the north, the woods of Fox Hill Park add a pleasant aspect. All these factors—the highways, the woods, and the school bus—played a role in the tragedy that occurred at 8:09 a.m., Monday, October 7.

One student who normally rode the bus was an eighth grader. Usually the thirteen-year-old boy (identity withheld) rose early and began his day at a neighborhood prayer meeting across the street from his home, then caught the bus to school. But on that Monday morning he did not attend the prayer gathering.

The week before, the boy had been caught eating candy on the school bus and had been suspended by the driver. An aunt offered to give the boy a ride, but that meant leaving early and missing the prayer meeting. And so a chain of events was set in motion that, before the day was over, would put the Nation's Capital into a full-blown state of terror.

Only a few days earlier, local police had assured area residents it was safe to send their children to school. But at 8:09 a.m., as the eighth grader climbed out of his aunt's car in front of the school, a single gunshot was heard. The boy was hit in the chest by a bullet from a high-powered rifle. Still alive, the thirteen-year-old was rushed to the Bowie Health Center. Realizing the child was close to death, doctors called nearby Andrews Air Force Base and had the boy airlifted by helicopter to the Washington Children's Hospital. The swift action proved decisive as surgeons were able to save the boy's life. Some five weeks later, he at last went home.

Back at the site of the shooting, police rushed to the scene and quickly focused on the wooded area adjacent to the school. In Fox Hill Park investigators found their most promising evidence to date. In the woods about one hundred fifty yards from where the boy had been hit, police discovered a spent shell casing and a patch of grass that had apparently been matted as the sniper lay in waiting. Then beside a fallen tree, police also discovered a chilling clue—a tarot card bearing the symbol of Death and the handwritten inscription, "Mister policeman, I am God."

As in some of the Montgomery County attacks, witnesses in Bowie reported seeing a white vehicle leaving the scene. But videotape from a red light camera at the nearest major intersection yielded no results. Once again, the gunman had struck and then escaped near a highway interchange with access to several major roads.

Normal life in the Nation's Capital now came to an end.

Area schools went to "Code Blue" alert status, canceling all outdoor activities, holding recess indoors, locking down all buildings and drawing all window blinds. Some schools taped black construction paper over their windows. In the days that followed, a *Washington Post* poll found that six out of ten parents limited their children's activities, one in four limited their school attendance, and one in six were keeping their kids off the school bus. High school football games were canceled or played at undisclosed locations up to one hundred fifty miles away. Many schools were forced to cancel their annual homecoming parades

and dances. Youth league soccer practices and games were canceled across the entire region.

With sniper attacks in four jurisdictions—Montgomery and
Prince George's counties in Maryland, the District of Columbia,
and Spotsylvania County, Virginia—area police formed a task
force to coordinate their efforts. Montgomery County Police
Headquarters was chosen to house the task force and was soon
encamped by the national media.

In the weeks to follow, Montgomery County Police Chief
Charles A. Moose would become a familiar figure to Americans
everywhere. But on the day of the shooting at Benjamin Tasker
Middle School, as the life of a thirteen-year-old eighth grader
hung in the balance, Moose faced the television cameras with
tears in his eyes. The sniper, he declared, had "crossed the line."

Chapter Three

The Middle School

and the Things We Value: Tolerance

Though I have driven many times past the interchange at Route 50 and Route 197 in Bowie, Maryland, I never noticed Benjamin Tasker Middle School. Now that I have seen pictures in the newspaper, it seems like a well-kept school in a pleasant neighborhood, a lot like suburban schools all over the country—a lot like the schools I attended. Only the awful scene of senseless shooting has brought it to national attention. Benjamin Tasker Middle School is where, on October 7, 2002, the D.C. Sniper attacked his only juvenile victim.

At 8:09 a.m. a thirteen-year-old student (identity withheld) was climbing out of his aunt's car outside the school. A single shot hit the boy in the chest and penetrated his abdomen. Taken first to the local health center, his life was saved when a helicopter from Andrews Air Force Base airlifted the boy to the Washington Children's Hospital.

As we have learned since 9/11, our communities are full of everyday heroes—like the emergency medical personnel who transported the stricken boy and the doctors who ultimately saved him. The roll of heroes also includes his teachers at Benjamin Tasker Middle School, many of whom have labored long and faithfully with few thanks or rewards.

I am grateful for the dedicated teachers of my own youth, and grateful we continue to have dedicated teachers today. That at least has remained the same. But as even educators agree, our schools have changed over the past generation. Why? Society has changed, families have changed and, as a result, so have our young people. They are a reflection of us.

SHOTS IN THE DARK

Not Giving Offense

Schools, then, reflect what we value. And schools in the Washington suburbs, like any major metropolitan area, have changed, too. When I was a thirteen-year-old in eighth grade, my school was a *junior* high school; after ninth grade I would enter the *senior* high school. Today most eighth graders attend *middle* schools. The early teen years are an awkward age when young people need special attention. So the idea of a junior and senior high, and the connotation that one is subordinate to the other, has fallen out of favor.

Today when I drive down Arlington Boulevard and look at my old alma mater, over the school entrance I can still see where the letters "Kenmore Middle School" once spelled "Kenmore Junior High School." The school has changed in another way, perhaps just as symbolic of our values today. In the Seventies, I proudly wore the green and gold of the Kenmore Braves. Today's football team takes the field as the Kenmore Cougars.

I do not mourn the change. Consideration for the feelings of others is a good thing. If racial caricatures such as Indian mascots are offensive to those being stereotyped, I believe the Christian response is to "give none offence ... even as I please all men in all things, not seeking mine own profit, but the profit of many, that they may be saved" (1 Corinthians 10:32-33). What is important is to not turn people away from Christ by offending them in matters unrelated to the gospel, "giving no offence in any thing, that the ministry be not blamed" (2 Corinthians 6:3). To offend people unnecessarily is "seeking mine own profit" by indulging in the satisfaction of deliberately hurting others.

Now, I am a *huge* Washington Redskins fan! My family got season tickets in the early Sixties before the team became popular, so I went to games at D.C. Stadium—now RFK Stadium—throughout my youth. Sonny Jurgensen, Charley Taylor, Bobby Mitchell, Sam Huff and many more were my boyhood heroes. Yet if the team were renamed, in time we would get over it. Men my age who grew up cheering for Johnny Unitas and the Baltimore Colts have, though they swore they never would, gotten used to the rooting for the Ravens. And when the NBA Washington Bullets became the Wizards, I applauded the owner's concern that urban violence not be glorified.

In the same vein, I learned early in my Washington career that it would be worth my life if I ever called female co-workers "girls" instead of "women" (or ever suggest they make coffee). Are

Washington women sensitive about that? Yes. Does it cost me anything, or compromise any important principles, to avoid giving offense? No.

The Core Issue

Some aspects of my boyhood days are better left behind. The world is better off without Speedy Gonzales or the Frito Bandito, without Polish jokes or lawn jockeys.

Yet when our schools today emphasize *tolerance* as a virtue for our children to learn, it goes beyond teaching consideration for others. It stems from a philosophy that my choices are valid for me and your choices are equally valid for you. So long as you and I do not hurt anyone else, we have the right to make our own choices and feel good about them. Or rather, we have a right to feel good about ourselves, and no one can be allowed to take that away from us.

Over the past generation, concerns about our public education system have ranged from values clarification and guided imagery to school-based health clinics, whole-language reading methods, ebonics and bilingual instruction, multiculturalism and globalism. I do not minimize these concerns. But it seems to me that the core issue is more basic.

Our schools reflect our society, and our society rejects the concept, found in the Bible, of the total depravity of man. People are innately good and ultimately perfectable. Human happiness occurs through individual self-actualization. Since people are unhappy when they feel guilty, the answer is not to stop the behavior that causes the guilt. Instead, the answer is to remove the guilt from the behavior. The idea of objective "sin" or "wickedness" is outmoded. If all of us learn tolerance then all of us can feel good about ourselves.

We do not need a Savior, for we can save ourselves from the unhappiness that besets us. So the alcoholic learns to love himself, rather than love God and despise himself. And the middle schooler is warned against drug use and early sex, not because they are biblically and socially wrong, but only because they are self-destructive and decrease personal happiness.

School Pictures

When I was a boy in the Sixties and Seventies, there were no Christian schools. We had Catholic parochial schools, but the only "Christian school" I knew was a small building on the way to my dentist in Arlington. The idea of a Christian school seemed strange to most people, who often whispered that it must have been started for white families to avoid integration. The Christian school movement as we know it today did not exist until I was in college, while the home school movement did not emerge until the Eighties.

Sending my own children to Christian schools in the Washington area was hard for my parents to understand. They sent *me* to public schools. Why would I pay tuition and drive my kids to school in Beltway traffic, when the local public school was free and provided bus transportation? And was the Christian school academically sound, especially when they put the Bible in every subject?

By the time my own kids were old enough for school, however, I could see that things had changed since I was a child. For me, there was one thing that summarized the difference. It was not the issue of, say, school prayer. While I lament the Supreme Court decision, it was issued the year that I started kindergarten, and so I never knew prayer in schools. Instead, it was something very mundane.

In my home office, the top shelf of my bookcase is reserved for memorabilia—old yearbooks, school newspapers, and an album my mother kept of my "School Days." There are sections for kindergarten through high school—report cards, drawings, special awards, class assignments, all were saved with loving care.

In elementary school back then, each year we would have a class picture taken. Perhaps schools still do that. Today as I look at those old pictures, beginning with my kindergarten class of 1963, staring back at me are girls in dresses and party shoes, and boys in bow ties and sweaters. We were dressed up for picture day. But our standard attire was still dresses for girls and dress clothes for boys. Even in junior high and high school, there was still a distinction between "school clothes" and "after-school clothes."

Now fast forward, thirty years in the future. I am just starting my daily commute on a warm, late-summer morning in September. I see the neighborhood kids walking to school. No dress clothes and party shoes here. Boys and girls look much the same. Jeans or shorts. Sneakers. Tee shirts and sweats.

To the best of my knowledge, casual clothes do not serve an academic purpose. Many schools are considering uniforms because studies suggest these *improve* student performance. So what is the reason? Again, our schools and our kids reflect us. And we do not like outside constraints being imposed on us. We may understand the need for discipline, but we value self-expression even more.

Playing the Game

As the sniper's reign of terror gripped the Washington area in October 2002, schools responded by holding recess indoors and canceling outdoor athletic practices and games. Even high school football games were canceled. That is serious! I know, because I played varsity football, and it remains one of the most exciting and rewarding experiences of my life.

When I was a boy playing youth sports in the Sixties, teams had cuts. In baseball I barely made it, yet learned the important lesson of how to ride the bench, pay my dues, and wait my turn. Football was a different story. It was *my* sport. To my mind, football is the ultimate team game. Success in football requires cooperation as well as aggressive and determined play. It paid off my senior year in high school when we won the district championship. I started at left guard and made the key touchdown block in the championship game. Those days of pep rallies, marching bands, homecomings, bonfires, and cheering fans are among the sweetest memories I have.

The rallies, homecomings, bonfires, and fans are still there. In many ways, however, the game has changed as society has changed. We see it in the professional ranks but, having followed football for nearly forty years, I have seen the changes even more at the youth level.

What has changed? Back in the dark ages, coaches were not expected to play every sub. If you were not a starter then you honed your game in practice, rode the bench that season, and looked forward to next year when you could compete for a starting spot. You paid your dues and waited your turn. Neither would a player *ask* for a water break. The philosophy was, "No whining, just put on your chin strap and get back on the field." Maybe that is not such a bad outlook on life.

When I look back at old team photos, I usually see five or six dads who helped with the coaching or equipment. Two or three mothers would coach the cheerleaders, while the other moms made banners and posters and snacks for after the game. And on those glorious autumn days when game time arrived, even at the youth league level, people from the surrounding community would come out to watch and cheer.

And then there were the guys I played with. By the time I played left guard for the mighty Generals of Washington-Lee High School, three of us lineman had played together since youth football. The quarterback and running backs had been my teammates since junior high. We had all paid our dues—together—and now it was our turn. We were rewarded with a championship. And whenever we scored a touchdown, our coaches told us that true sportsmen did their jobs quietly and handed the ball to the referee.

The first year my own son played football, I volunteered to coach. My father had done the same for me. But I soon found out that times had changed.

The boys were not shy about telling *me* what positions *they* wanted to play. They expected significant playing time in every game or they might quit. Practices could not go overtime since parents were on tight schedules. My game day responsibilities included arranging rides for boys whose parents did not attend. The awards dinner was a casual affair since only three boys had neckties. And I doubt that, in the mobile society of today, many of my players were still together in high school.

Of course, my grandparents probably rolled their eyes in the Fifties when my mother and father were teenagers. And no doubt my parents could not understand my generation in the Seventies. Kids today have qualities—inquisitiveness, independent thinking, expressiveness—that God can use if channeled in the right direction. But there is no denying that, not just in young people (who are reflections of their parents) but in society at large, there is a greater emphasis today on *self*.

Cultivating Christ-Esteem

The concept of self-esteem is a controversial topic in the church today. These are deep waters, and I do not pretend to resolve them here. On the one hand, Christians are called to "follow after ... things wherewith one may edify another" (Romans 14:19) and to speak only "that which is good to the use of edifying, that it may minister grace unto the hearers" (Ephesians 4:29). If that is the case, do not we *want* to build self-esteem in other people? After all, "Pleasant words are as an honeycomb, sweet to the soul, and health to the bones" (Proverbs 16:24). I know that I have sought to develop in my children a sense of confidence in themselves—to be like The Little Engine That Could who chugged, "I think I can, I think I can."

I do not agree with people who say, "You must love yourself before you can love others!" But is it necessary to *hate* yourself before you can love others? In a sense, it *is* necessary. Only by hating ourselves can we see our need for a Savior, and only by giving our lives to that Savior can we know *His* love and show it to others.

What we need before *self-esteem* is, as Don Matzat says in the title of his classic book, *Christ-esteem*. He explains that, because we as born-again believers have experienced a double birth, we also lead a double life. "We were born into the world in Adam, and the old nature of Adam was joined to us," Matzat points out. "As a result of coming to faith in Jesus Christ through the hearing of the gospel, we were born again in Christ Jesus, and the life of Christ was joined to us."

We contain within ourselves *two* sources of life, what the New Testament calls "the old man" and "the new man," or the flesh (our sinful human nature) and the Spirit (Christ living within us). "Because of this double life," Matzat continues, "the normal Christian experience is conflict. Attempting to change our natural earthly life and become more loving, kind, self-controlled, and considerate is a hopeless task. Our human life will not cooperate with our desire for self-improvement." In Romans 7:18-25, Paul describes this conflict.

> For I know that in me (that is, in my flesh,) dwelleth no good thing: for to will is present with me; but how to perform that which is good I find not. For the good that I would I do not: but the evil which I would not, that I do. Now if I do that I would not, it is no more I that do it, but sin that dwelleth in me. I find then a law, that, when I would do good, evil is present with me. For I delight in the law of God after the inward man: But I see another law in my members, warring against the law of my mind, and bringing me into captivity to the law of sin which is in my members. O wretched man that I am! who shall deliver me from the body of this death? I thank God through Jesus Christ our Lord. So then with the mind I myself serve the law of God; but with the flesh the law of sin.

What Really Edifies

Here perhaps is an answer to our dilemma, How can self-esteem be *wrong* when Christians are *supposed* to desire the building up of other people?

Efforts to foster self-esteem are unprofitable when they attempt to build up "the old man" of the flesh, to bolster the old sinful human nature. Christ-esteem is to build up "the new man" of the Spirit, to cultivate greater conformity to the image of Christ. As Christians we *do* want to "follow after ... things wherewith one may edify another" and speak only "that which is good to the use of edifying, that it may minister grace unto the hearers."

But what is the definition of "edifying" others? True edification is not building up the old sinful nature but rather strengthening each other for closer communion with Christ.

Only thus can a man find the power to overcome his enslavement to a sinful nature, not by looking *into* himself but by turning *away*— and turning *toward* Christ. " [T]hey which live should not henceforth live unto themselves, but unto him which died for them, and rose again ... Therefore if any man be in Christ, he is a new creature." (2 Corinthians 5:15,17). "For ye are dead, and your life is hid with Christ in God" (Colossians 3:3).

And who is this Christ? He is the One who "hath blessed us with all spiritual blessings in heavenly places in Christ" (Ephesians 1:3); who "according as his divine power hath given unto us all things that pertain unto life and godliness" (2 Peter 1:3); who "of God is made unto us wisdom, and righteousness, and sanctification, and redemption" (1 Corinthians 1:30); and through whom "ye are complete in him, which is the head of all principality and power" (Colossians 2:9-10).

A Difficult Admission

The D.C. Sniper shootings horrified the nation because of the threat to life and safety, and to our way of life. But the attacks have also challenged our basic assumption about human nature. Today we believe that, because people are basically good, it is possible to live in communities made harmonious by a mutual tolerance for everyone's self-absorption. This is a false hope.

To understand what I mean, let us take a case from modern history. We find it comforting to believe that Adolf Hitler was an aberration, that he was either mad or demonic. If mad, then he was abnormal and not one of us. If demonic, then again he is not one of us but rather a supernatural phenomenon. We look for ways to explain his aberration—that (among current theories) Hitler witnessed the rape of his mother; contracted syphilis from a French prostitute in World War I; over-compensated for having a rumored Jewish grandfather; saw his mother killed by the malpractice of a Jewish doctor; was a repressed homosexual.

Somehow we cannot face the fact that Adolf Hitler was a man like us. To say so is to admit the possibility that anyone we know—that we ourselves—could become a Hitler. Such an admission is too terrible to make. But it is true. And in the same way, the thought of a sniper cold-bloodedly murdering his victims from a distance (and isn't that what Hitler did?) is an unwelcome reminder of the dark side of human nature.

Despite our modernity, our world is still capable of Adolf Hitler and the Holocaust, of Osama Bin Laden and suicide bombers, of Ted Bundy and the D.C. Sniper—and of all the countless brutal crimes that take place in our cities every day without making the headlines. Can we still say that human nature is basically good? And if not, is our quest for "self" an exercise in anything but futility?

Some people criticize the Christian faith and its doctrine of the total depravity of man as being negative and mentally unhealthy. In fact, the Bible offers our best and only hope. The Word of God "tells it like it is," faces the truth we do not want to admit, and then provides the only possible solution:

> *"For since by man [Adam] came death, by man [the incarnate Christ] came also the resurrection of the dead. For as in Adam all die, even so in Christ shall all be made alive. (1 Corinthians 15:21-22)*

10.09.02

Prince William County, Va. — Bullet fragments taken from a customer fatally shot at a service station in Prince William County on Wednesday evening were conclusively linked yesterday to the sniper who now has claimed seven lives in nine days and has changed the way the Washington region goes about its everyday chores. Although authorities had suspected all along that the sniper was responsible for the death of Dean Harold Meyers, 53, a Gaithersburg [Maryland] engineer, they confirmed it only after ballistics tests ...

Again the awful pattern repeated itself. At 8:18 p.m., Wednesday, October 9, two days after the shooting at Benjamin Tasker Middle School, the sniper struck again. Once more the gunman chose a site within view of a major highway interchange. But this time, there were two horrifying differences.

First, where the middle school attack occurred on the extreme eastern edge of the Washington metro area, the October 9 killing hit the western edge. By targeting two sites in two days that are almost exact geographic opposites, it seemed as if the murderer was making a statement. The second difference? Unlike two days earlier, this time the shooting was fatal.

Dean Harold Meyers, 53, had worked late that evening. A civil engineer, he was a "solid, conscientious man" who stayed until the job was done. Meyers had worked twenty years for the same company, making the long commute each day from his townhouse in Gaithersburg, Maryland, to his office near Manassas, Virginia.

The trip home that night would traverse some of the worse traffic bottlenecks in the Washington area, a total of some thirty-five miles along I-66, the Capital Beltway, and I-270. Many area commuters who are delayed in leaving work at their regular time do, in fact, put off their drive home until rush hour is over.

With a long drive ahead of him, Meyers stopped for gas at the Sunoco station on 7203 Sudley Road in Prince William County, Virginia, just north of the city of Manassas. It was a little past eight and night had fallen. But Sudley Road was brightly lit by the many retail stores and gas stations that line the multi-lane divided roadway. Directly across the street from the Sunoco is a large shopping center and parking lot. Less than a thousand feet to the right is the entrance for I-66.

At 8:18 p.m. as Meyers finished pumping gas and prepared to get back in his black Mazda, he was gunned down by a sniper's bullet. Meyers had been an army master sergeant and decorated Vietnam veteran, a man who had nearly lost an arm in combat. He had survived his wounds and, through years of physical therapy, regained its use. With the D.C. Sniper, however, he had no second chance.

As before, the gunman escaped without detection. Frustratingly, the owner of the Sunoco had purchased security cameras two weeks earlier but had not yet located someone to install them. A videotape might have enabled police to reconstruct the trajectory of the bullet and deduce where the sniper had been located.

Some observers noted that a Michaels Arts and Crafts store was located across the street from the Sunoco and speculated about a connection. Twenty-two Michaels outlets are located in the Washington area, including one near Benjamin Tasker Middle School. Others pointed out that three shootings took place near Radio Shack stores, and still others discounted any connections since all the attacks occurred in areas with a large retail presence. And again, witnesses reported seeing a white van being driven erratically after the shooting.

With the killing in Prince William County, five jurisdictions were now involved in the case. Amid all the speculation, however, the task force was determined one thing would be sure. Next time authorities would be ready with a rapid response.

Chapter Four

The Gas Station
and the Things We Value: Autonomy

When the news came on October 9, 2002, I did not need to watch the television. Dean Harold Meyers had been shot by a sniper while pumping gas at the Sunoco station on Sudley Road and I-66 near Manassas, Virginia. I did not need to watch TV, for I knew that gas station well. I had filled my own car at that Sunoco many times, and recently too. Until a few years ago I lived in the same county and worked just a few blocks away.

As a boy growing up in Washington, the idea of ever living or working near Manassas would have seemed ridiculous. Manassas was not even considered part of the Washington metropolitan area. Our world encompassed downtown Washington—where my father, like most other fathers, worked—and the nearer Virginia suburbs of Arlington, Falls Church, Alexandria, Annandale, and (when the shopping malls were built) Tysons Corner and Vienna.

To us, Maryland was another state. And the "outer" Virginia suburbs of my day were places I encountered only as a high school football player. Dulles Airport and the planned community of Reston, with their modern architectural designs, seemed like the New York World's Fair transplanted to the Virginia horse country. And Manassas? That was a place we read about in school, in our Virginia history books. It was a place my grandparents would take me for a Saturday drive into the country.

Grandma and Grandpa were both from the South. They loved to tell me stories of our gallant heroes in gray, stories they heard firsthand from their own grandparents. And as a boy I loved to hear these stories. Even in the Virginia suburbs of Washington, the sense of Southern heritage is still very real. I attended Stonewall Jackson Elementary School and Washington-Lee High School. Arlington County, where I grew up, was named for General Lee's estate. The main roads are Arlington Boulevard, Lee Highway, and Jefferson Davis Highway.

So my main connection to Manassas was a place for daytrips, a place where I could visit the battlefield and my grandparents would reverently repeat the famous words, "There stands Jackson like a stone wall! Rally to the Virginian!" And then we could stand on the very spot where history had been made.

Back then, we could not have imagined a sniper attack in Manassas. The intersection of Sudley Road and I-66 did not exist. There was no interstate highway near Manassas. The sprawl of gas stations, stores, and two shopping malls that stand there today had not been built.

Today, I understand very well why Manassas would be the target of a domestic terrorist. Suburban growth in the area has been intense. Pitched battles have been fought over proposals to build a shopping center adjacent to Manassas National Battlefield, even to build a "Disney's America" history theme park just west of the town. Both proposal were defeated, but the growth continues.

Even more, I can understand why the sniper would target a gas station. Four of the fourteen shootings occurred at gas stations— the Sunoco in Manassas, an Exxon station in Fredericksburg, Virginia, and two stations in suburban Maryland. Why gas stations? They symbolize one of the things we value most in suburban America today—our autonomy, our right to be in control. The ability to fill our tanks is, in reality, the ability to control where we go, what we do, and when we do it.

Two-Car Families

Electric streetcars were still running in downtown Washington when I was born, though I do not remember riding one. But I do remember seeing the tracks still embedded in the roadways. And though the streetcars ultimately gave way to the emerging car culture of the Fifties and Sixties, in my youth it was still unusual for a family to have more than one car.

When my wife Donna was a girl in the Virginia suburbs, her mother would wake up the family, prepare breakfasts and pack lunches, help her husband get ready for work, then drive him to the bus stop. Since they had only one car, she would use it for errands during the day and pick up her husband at the bus stop each night. In my family we had the opposite arrangement. Dad would take the family car to work each morning and mom would stay home to watch the children. If she wanted to attend her Tuesday morning ladies bowling league, she might get a ride by offering to babysit for a friend. When I was old enough to ride a bike, she had a basket installed over the back tire so I go to the neighborhood store for milk and bread.

Today, few suburbanites would put up with such restrictions. Though Donna decided to stay at home with our children, she made it quite clear that she would *not* be stuck without a car! I could not blame her. In today's suburbs it simply is not possible to do most of your shopping within the neighborhood. And by the time our own children were born, Donna was virtually alone in our neighborhood during the day. In Washington, most mothers had taken their cars and driven to their own jobs—some of them, ironically, to help make their car payments and buy their gas. There was no Tuesday morning ladies bowling league, no mothers to trade babysitting for carpooling, no neighborhood support network of any kind. Donna definitely needed a car.

Being honest, I too was unwilling to do without a car. Once I tried commuting to work on the Metro system, but could stand it for only a week or so. The worst part of public transportation was not the pushing and crowding or anything like that. The worst part was, I had to *wait!* I was not in control. At least in my own car I could leave when I wanted, always be assured of having a seat, listen to my own music, have a feeling of control.

Traffic might be heavy but I could plan for it, could choose different routes to get around it. I did not have to depend on anyone else. Many fellow commuters must have felt the same because—even though Washington traffic jams are rated the second worst in the nation behind only Los Angeles—most people refuse to abandon their cars. Just look around at rush hour. Nearly every car has a single driver, while the HOV lanes (reserved for "high occupancy vehicles") are almost empty. Suburban commuters know the roads are jammed, but they still choose the autonomy of their own cars.

Our Gas-Guzzling Fantasies

As mentioned earlier, I enjoy writing for business journals. Believe it or not, I actually wrote an article once about the history of the humble gas station.

The mom-and-pop filling station is long gone. No more attendants in white suits, caps, and bow ties who offer to check your oil and wash your windows. When self-service gasoline came along in the late Sixties and early Seventies, neighborhood convenience stores

43

could install a couple of pumps in their parking lots. To compete, gas stations converted their service bays into convenience stores.

The Eighties brought an emphasis on high volume as gas stations installed multiple fuel islands to boost traffic and sales. Today's state-of-the-art station not only generates high traffic but draws customers with a large, attractive, brightly lit store that may include traditional convenience items, a fastfood restaurant and drive-thru, deli sandwiches and pizza to go, and of course an ATM. The gas pump accepts your credit card or scans your keychain pass, asks if you want a car wash, and may even have a video screen that starts to play when you activate the pump.

Gas stations have changed, however, because cars and drivers have changed. When I was a boy, gasoline cost a quarter a gallon. But even in a suburb of a major city, there were few places our family wanted or needed to go other than downtown or in our immediate community. As a high schooler I bought my first gallon of gas for fifty-eight cents, yet I seldom needed to drive much farther than school. What family could ever need more than two cars? And when the oil embargoes hit, we had even more reason to keep close to home.

The suburbs are much different today. Families with three or even four cars are common—one each for mom and dad and the teens. When I was a teenager, my father and mother did "chaffeur duty" as part of their parental responsibility. When I did the same for my own children, I was the oddball father who would not let my kids have a car. Thoughts of fuel economy now seem as obsolete as the fifty-five-mile-per-hour national speed limit. Sales of SUVs, minivans, and light pickups far outstrip those of ordinary passenger cars. Advertisements, which once boasted of miles per gallon, today emphasize power, speed, luxury, roominess.

In TV commercials today, SUV owners are seen experiencing their wildest driving fantasies. They drive through forests, climb mountains, drive up sheer canyon walls. They go wherever they want, even without roads, in the quest for personal space, fulfillment, autonomy. Never mind that SUVs have far more horsepower than needed for suburban commuting or that off-road capability is not required for trips to the mall. And if gas prices go up this summer? Today we resent any restriction on our right to go when and where we please. We expect our politicians to go after the price gougers, not to tell us that we should drive less or suggest we get rid of our gas-guzzlers.

How Autonomous Are We?

The Manassas Sunoco does a brisk business because it provides what customers want. It is convenient to major roads and located just off the interstate. You can gas and go, then be on your way. You are in control.

Perhaps that is why our culture has a major problem with the claims of Jesus Christ. He demands that we yield control of our lives to Him. He requires that whatever we do, wherever we go, we first seek His guidance and approval. What does Jesus have to offer, what relevance does He have, for a culture that views personal autonomy as a right? That believes being in control is a prerequisite for a satisfying life?

First, let us check our assumptions. Are we as "in control" as we think? The three vehicles in the driveway require hundreds of dollars each month in payments. The garage to put them in, and the house to go with it, cost hundreds more. To afford cars and houses, many families must send both mother and father to work—and pay large sums of money for people to watch their children. In many suburban families today the routine is: get up, go to work, come home after dark, spend the evening doing chores and errands, go to bed.

How much autonomy do we really have? The daily routine of rushing off to school or day care, commuting to work, impressing the boss with our late hours, beating the traffic home—it is like a intricate web that we weave. How easily it can all unravel! Even when we seem to have things under control, there is still the underlying sense that we are just barely staying ahead. One mishap—an accident ties up traffic, our daycare provider moves away, our child gets sick, we need to call a plumber, our credit limit is exceeded, our economy goes into recession—can threaten the whole fabric of our lives. We break down, we are vulnerable.

Autonomy or Sufficiency?

Our autonomy, then, is a false autonomy. Modern suburbia offers a sense of control. But in reality, our lives today are more interdependent than ever on a network of support systems.

What does Jesus have to offer? Consider an experience in the life of the apostle Paul.

[T]here was given to me a thorn in the flesh . . .

Here we learn, in 2 Corinthians 12:7-10, that Paul contracted a serious physical impairment. Scholars theorize ailments from epilepsy to eye trouble. The unexpected had entered his life but he had a recourse.

For this thing I besought the Lord thrice, that it might depart from me.

Paul tapped into a support system that he knew would not fail him. He prayed for deliverance from his situation and, though Paul did not receive the answer he at first sought, his God lovingly provided an even better solution.

And he said unto me, My grace is sufficient for thee: for my strength is made perfect in weakness. Most gladly therefore will I rather glory in my infirmities, that the power of Christ may rest upon me.

The apostle yielded control over his situation to God, willingly and not out of compulsion. In surrendering his autonomy to God—in forsaking the ultimately futile drive to master his world—Paul gained in return something far better. He gained sufficiency, God's sufficiency, to carry him through. Far from losing control, Paul could exclaim,

Therefore I take pleasure in infirmities, in reproaches, in necessities, in persecutions, in distresses for Christ's sake: for when I am weak, then am I strong.

Grace is the Key

What alternative puts us in a position of greater control over our circumstances: Clinging to our own false sense of autonomy? Or yielding to God's sufficiency? If by *control* we mean the ability to rise above our circumstances, to not let our trials overcome us, then sufficiency is more effective than autonomy.

And what is this "sufficiency"? God declared to Paul, "My grace is sufficient for thee." So it is grace that supplies the sufficiency we need. But what is this grace? The Bible has much to say on this topic.

Grace can best be understood as "unmerited favor," something we receive without deserving it or working for it. Salvation in Christ is the best example. Because "all have sinned" (Romans 3:23), because "there is none righteous" (Romans 3:10), we deserve death and not heaven. Can we then work to earn our salvation? No, because "to him that worketh is the reward not reckoned of grace, but of debt" and "if it be of works, then it is no more grace" (Romans 4:4, 11:6).

Most people in the world today believe that salvation can be earned through work, through enough good deeds to somehow out-weigh the bad. But if that were true, Christ's death on the cross as payment for our sins would not be necessary. "I do not frustrate the grace of God: for if righteousness come by the law, then Christ is dead in vain" (Galatians 2:21). Instead we read in the scriptures that "through the grace of the Lord Jesus Christ we shall be saved" (Acts 15:11) and that we are "justified freely by his grace through the redemption that is in Christ Jesus" (Romans 3:24).

Or read this: "For ye know the grace of our Lord Jesus Christ, that, though he was rich, yet for your sakes he became poor, that ye through his poverty might be rich" (2 Corinthians 8:9). Talk about unmerited favor! "For by grace are ye saved through faith; and that not of yourselves: it is the gift of God: not of works, lest any man should boast" (Ephesians 2:8-9). Salvation, then, is not a reward but a gift. To be obtained, a gift must be received. How? By faith that "we have redemption through his blood, the forgiveness of sins, according to the riches of his grace" (Ephesians 1:7).

Grace Under Pressure

But wait, there is more. To the harried suburbanite, to the man or woman who is struggling to keep pace in the fast lane, there is more good news. For the person who has placed his trust in Christ, grace is also available to meet the trials and troubles of our lives right here, right now.

> *Thou therefore, my son, be strong in the grace that is in Christ Jesus. (2 Timothy 2:1)*

> *Let us therefore come boldly unto the throne of grace, that we may obtain mercy, and find grace to help in time of need. (Hebrews 4:16)*

> *And God is able to make all grace abound toward you; that ye, always having all sufficiency in all things, may abound to every good work. (2 Corinthians 9:8)*

> *Wherefore we receiving a kingdom which cannot be moved, let us have grace, whereby we may serve God acceptably with reverence and godly fear. (Hebrews 12:28)*

Strength and grace under pressure. Help in time of need. Sufficiency in all things. A kingdom that cannot be moved. What wonderful comforts these have been to me—when I was stuck on I-95, when the boss nixed my project, when I had an activity scheduled every single night of the week, when the bills mounted at the end of the month.

How about you? Autonomy—or sufficiency? Remember that question the next time you hit every stoplight red or get in the slow line at the fastfood counter. When we get angry the real cause is our wounded pride at not being in control. And that is the time to remember,

God resisteth the proud, but giveth grace unto the humble" (James 4:6).

10.11.02

Spotsylvania County, Va. — A Philadelphia man was fatally shot at a Spotsylvania County gas station [Friday] as a state police trooper investigated a traffic accident across the street, launching a massive and frustrating search for the sniper who claimed his eighth victim in the Washington area over the past 10 days. Law enforcement sources said last night that ballistic evidence conclusively links the shooting of Kenneth H. Bridges, 53, to the sniper who has killed seven others and wounded two in the Washington region — each time slipping away undetected. This time, a Virginia state trooper, who was only 50 yards away from Bridges at the time of the 9:30 a.m. attack, heard a gunshot and ran to help, but never saw the shooter . . .

"With a uniformed trooper directly across the street, we're obviously dealing with an individual who is extremely violent and doesn't care," said Major Howard Smith of the Spotsylvania sheriff's office as he described the eleventh sniper shooting. Only thirty-six hours after the last slaying, the killer once again targeted a gas station near an interstate highway ramp—this time, while a Virginia state trooper was within fifty yards of scene.

The victim, Kenneth Bridges, 53, was only four hours from his home in Philadelphia when he stopped for gas at the Massaponax Exit off Interstate 95. He had rented a silver Buick for a business trip and, on that Friday morning, October 11, he could hope to be with his family by mid afternoon. A father of six, he was a leader in Philadelphia's African-American business community and had founded a national product distribution network for black-owned manufacturers.

Bridges chose the middle island of the Exxon station on Route 1, fourteen hundred feet from the reentry ramp onto I-95. The two roads parallel each other at that point, providing egress for Lee's Hill, a major residential development. The area around the ramp offers an array of gas stations, restaurants and fast food, plus a discount mini-mall and a multiplex movie theater.

At 9:30 a.m., at the sound of a single gunshot, the state trooper ran to help. Bridges was shot in the upper torso and died on the scene. The trooper did not see the shooter, but two witnesses saw a white Chevy Astro van turn south on Route 1 as the shot was fired, heading toward the interstate. Other witnesses reported a white Ford Econo van. In both cases, a ladder rack was seen on roof of the vehicle.

Minutes after the slaying, authorities were ready with a massive response. Traffic was stopped at major highways between Fredericksburg and Washington, creating huge backups that lasted for hours. Officers with automatic weapons and wearing bullet-proof jackets inspected every vehicle. Police spotters were stationed on bridges and overpasses. White vans, literally by the hundreds, were pulled over and searched. Yet no suspects were apprehended.

The day after the October 11 killing police released a composite sketch of the white van reported by witnesses, plus a sketch of the white box truck allegedly seen in connection with the original Montgomery County attacks. But even as police decided to go public with the sketches, authorities also worried the lead might prove a dead end and provide cover for the gunman. The white van seen after the Manassas shooting, for example, turned out to be unrelated. White vans were now drawing so much attention, investigators acknowledged that people might be prone to deliberately look for them.

Explaining the dilemma, Virginia State Police Superintendent W. Gerald Massengill said, "I wouldn't want the people of Virginia to focus just on white vans. We do not want preconceived notions out there. But certainly ... you have to play the hand that you're dealt. And the information that has come to us deals with white vans. So we're still interested in white vans."

As it was, up to one thousand calls per hour were overwhelming a toll-free hotline staffed by sixty FBI agents. In Prince William County alone, police received tips from thirteen thousand callers in the thirty-six hours following the Manassas shooting.

Yet police had few real leads to go on. Virginia police checked guest registries of motels located near the three shootings in their state. An employee of a Howard Johnson's reported seeing a white van being driven by a blond woman with a man in the passenger seat, shortly before the Massaponax slaying. And police with bloodhounds investigated a room at a Ramada hotel and questioned a man who had recently stayed there, but discovered nothing of interest. The man, a Caucasian with sandy hair and a mustache, matched a "tentative description" of the shooter. "They said I looked like the picture of someone at another shooting," he told reporters. Several other men fitting the description were also detained and released.

At task force headquarters, Chief Moose asked the public to report anyone who exhibited anger toward police and expressed "some sort of satisfaction" in the killings, especially if they were growing agitated and becoming irregular in their work attendance or daily schedule. Other investigators acknowledged to the media that the pattern of attacks now suggested the sniper might be methodically scouting locations, planning targets, and mapping escape routes. As one source speculated, "It could be a hunter's mentality."

The effects of the sniper shootings were now rippling throughout the entire Washington metropolitan region. The governor of Maryland suggested National Guard troops might be summoned on Election Day to protect polling places. And with Halloween coming, several municipalities canceled planned celebrations. The town of Vienna, Virginia, called off its annual parade for the first time in fifty-six years. Other jurisdictions canceled "spook house" events as being in bad taste. Two farms in rural Maryland each reported being stuck with more than fifty thousand dollars in unsold pumpkins. Another farm in a Virginia suburb spent two hundred thousand dollars to set up a petting zoo and life-size Candyland, only to have two hundred groups cancel their reservations.

Many retail stores in Montgomery County, site of the first seven shootings, reported that business was down by fifty percent. Officials estimated that county-wide economic activity was off by up to twenty-five percent. Tourist groups canceled sightseeing excursions to the Nation's Capital. Tour bus companies reported numerous cancellations. One hotel in Fairfax, Virginia, saw occupancy plunge from eighty to forty-five percent. By contrast, grocery delivery services and window-blind companies witnessed a surge in sales.

And at Massaponax High School, just a few miles from the Exxon station where Kenneth Bridges was slain, the homecoming dance scheduled for Saturday night was canceled. A sophomore interviewed by *The Washington Post* lamented, "I never thought I would be saying this, but this is like 9/11 all over again."

Chapter Five

The Interstate
and the Things We Value: Mobility

The words "Massaponax Exit" probably mean nothing to you. Even today, they mean nothing to most residents of the Washington area. News announcers must have consulted their Associated Press pronunciation guide in making their reports. But on October 11, 2002, when I heard the words "Massaponax Exit" on the nightly news, my attention was immediately riveted to the screen.

This was where my mother lives.

Just as incredibly to me, the D.C. Sniper had struck in Spotsylvania, Virginia, shooting and killing another random victim, Kenneth Bridges, at an Exxon station off Interstate 95. Traveling from his home in Philadelphia, Bridges had pulled off the highway at the Massaponax Exit to fill up his car with gas.

Spotsylvania and neighboring Fredericksburg are, like Manassas, names from my boyhood Virginia history books. The surrounding area was the site of pivotal Confederate victories at Fredericksburg and Chancellorsville, and later the awful carnage of The Wilderness. All three sites are now maintained by the National Park Service today, as is Stonewall Jackson Shrine just south of Spotsylvania where the storied general died after his greatest triumph.

In more recent times, Fredericksburg and Spotsylvania were the place my parents would take our family for weekend getaways in the country. Our favorite destination was a lodge with a duck pond and golf course on Route 3. Later, we almost bought an A-frame chalet at Lake of the Woods. Today, the lodge has been paved over for a shopping mall and Lake of the Woods sells timeshares.

Fredericksburg and Spotsylvania are still about an hour's drive south of the Washington area. But even if Massaponax is a name unfamiliar to most D.C. residents, they *all* know the name of

Interstate 95. I-95 is the new main street of metro Washington. Most commuters travel it every day. Our jobs and our homes are no longer downtown but largely in suburbs, suburbs that are now interconnected by I-95 and its tributaries. And these same roads have turned one-time country towns—from Fredericksburg, Virginia, to Frederick, Maryland—into satellite communities of the Nation's Capital.

The sniper's attack on Interstate 95 was an attack on the very lifeline of Washington. People across the entire region, even people who had never heard of the Massaponax Exit before, were terrified. Interstate 95 provides the mobility that makes suburban life possible.

Old Towns, New Starts

When my father died several years ago, my mother decided it would be best to buy a new home and start over. At the time she wanted to move far enough away to avoid city congestion but remain close to my sister and me who then lived in the Virginia suburbs. Remembering our old family excursions, I suggested Fredericksburg.

The move worked out great. Connected to metro Washington by Interstate 95 and no longer an isolated country town, Fredericksburg has added an upbeat cultural life to its rich Virginia heritage. But even in the years since my mother moved to a subdivision off the Massaponax Exit, development has boomed and traffic has increased. Now, sadly, even Fredericksburg and Spotsylvania County are united to the Nation's Capital through the awful tragedy of the D.C. Sniper.

I know the Massaponax Exit well, for I have driven it many times. I have often used the Exxon station where Kenneth Bridges was brutally murdered, and I have probably used the same pump on more than one occasion. So has my mother. It could have been either one of us. It could have been anyone in the Washington area who uses an I-95 exit. Why? Because from Fredericksburg to Frederick, every day we are all on the go.

The Pace Picks Up

When I first entered the ministry, for a time the Lord moved our family to another state. When God returned us to Washington and a new ministry, I could not believe how much the pace of life—always hectic in the Nation's Capital—had picked up! I was prepared for commuting. But now it seemed that even everyday activities, like shopping or going to church, required using an interstate or some other freeway. We could not go anywhere at less than the minimum forty-five miles an hour.

What a contrast from the suburbs of my youth. From our home in the Boulevard Manor subdivision of Arlington, just about everything we needed was on Wilson Boulevard. We seldom had to go any farther, at least for daily necessities. On one end of Wilson Boulevard was Seven Corners Shopping Center and its department stores. One the other end was Parkington Shopping Center. In between was our shoe store, our barber, our discount bread store. My mother usually shopped for groceries at the Grand Union, where she faithfully collected S&H Green Stamps. Each week she carefully pasted them into her stamp book. When it was filled, she could redeem it for a new blender, dishware set, or other rewards.

Now fast forward thirty years. Over that time, my own commutes reflected the influence of the interstate. For my first job, I commuted downtown as my father did. My next two jobs were both in Maryland, near Beltway exits. By the time our children were teenagers, we had purchased a home near I-95 because of its easy access to the far-flung necessities of our suburban lives.

And so, as only suburban commuters can understand, my life was dictated by the rhythms of the interstate. My home and job were thirty-five miles apart. Though I-95 was easily the most direct route, in the mornings I avoided it. Instead I took the back roads and side streets. Total travel time, seventy-five minutes. At the end of the day, I had my evening commute timed to the minute. If I hit it just right, before the HOV restrictions went into effect, I could be home in as little as forty-five minutes. But if somebody had a fender bender by the side of the road . . .

And that is only the half of it. Go to church? Take I-95. Shopping? I-95 or the Prince William Parkway. An away game for our kid's school? Again I-95. Baseball practice? Once again, I-95. Visit my mother in Fredericksburg? I-95. My mother-in-law in Springfield? Take I-95 to the Springfield Parkway. Dinner with my sister in Arlington? I-95 to I-395. Thanksgiving at my sister-in-law's house in Fairfax? I-95 to the Beltway.

You get the picture. Like most suburb dwellers, we were living life in the fast lane. We were getting our three thousand-mile oil changes every six weeks. Gas and car maintenance alone were running two hundred dollars a month. It seemed we could not go anywhere without using an interstate.

Pros and Cons

That brings us back to mobility. The interstate highway system has transformed the country. Urban, suburban, and exurban development has followed the highways. Most commerce in the United States is now shipped by truck. Visiting my grandparents in Florida once meant a tortuous and interminable drive along Route 1. Now the same trip can be done in a day. Tragically, Kenneth Bridges was only four hours from his home in Philadelphia.

Interstate 95 helped turn Fredericksburg and many other towns into growing communities (while towns that were bypassed have often fallen into decay). The interstates have provided Americans with more access to jobs and housing, to shopping and services— even as they have dispersed millions of families, including my own. For better or worse, the interstates have changed our lives by giving us unprecedented mobility.

Mobility helped me build my career, made it possible for me to take the best jobs I could find anywhere in the Washington area. My wife and I could buy an affordable house in a nice suburban neighborhood because the interstate made it accessible to work. But my life in the fast lane has also dictated my schedule and often left me exhausted, frustrated, harried, frantic.

With time on my hands during all those traffic jams, I have often thought about a seeming contradiction in the Christian life. If people today are constantly "on the go," does that imply restlessness— which in turn suggests discontent? Are we not commanded to "be still, and know that I am God" (Psalm 46:10)? Yet at the same time, as Christians we are told to "press toward the mark for the prize of the high calling of God in Christ Jesus" (Philippians 3:14). Paul himself admonished, "Know ye not that they which run in a race run all, but one receiveth the prize? So run, that ye may obtain" (1 Corinthians 9:24).

So which is it? To be still, or to press forward? To be content, or to run the race? More to the point, how can I know if my "hurry up" suburban life is pleasing to God?

Look at the "commute" that Paul had to *his* work. "In journeyings often, in perils of waters, in perils of robbers, in perils by mine own countrymen, in perils by the heathen, in perils in the city, in perils in the wilderness, in perils in the sea, in perils among false brethren; in weariness and painfulness, in watchings often, in hunger and thirst, in fastings often, in cold and nakedness" (2 Corinthians 11:26-27). That is a whole lot worse than anything I have ever encountered on the Beltway! Yet the apostle also enjoyed "the peace of God, which passeth all understanding" (Philippians 4:7).

How did he do it?

A Still Small Voice

"Let us run with patience the race that is set before us" (Hebrews 12:1). That is easy to say. But practically, if we have to run, how *do* we run with patience?

A man with whom I can identify is the prophet Elijah. In 1 Kings 19:9 we find him cowering in a cave, afraid for his life. But how could this be? This same Elijah had called down fire from heaven and slain the prophets of Baal. His prayers had ended a great drought, and twice he had been fed by angels. Yet Elijah was now on the go. He was running the race—but the wrong race, as he fled in fear from his earthly enemies.

No wonder God saw his flight to the cave and "said unto him, What doest thou here, Elijah?" Ironically, the cave was upon Mount Horeb, the same mount where Moses had come into the presence of God (Exodus 24:18). Yet the fact seemed lost on Elijah. Even when the voice of the Lord came to him, the prophet thought only of his troubles. "The children of Israel have forsaken Thy covenant," he sobbed, "thrown down thine altars, and slain Thy prophets with the sword; and I, even only I, am left; and they seek my life, to take it away" (19:10).

God tried to get Elijah's attention with a great wind, then an earthquake and fire that shook the mountain. Finally He spoke to the prophet in "a still small voice" (19:12), and at last Elijah began to listen. "And it was so, when Elijah heard it, that he wrapped his face in his mantle, and went out, and stood in the entering in of the cave" (19:13). God asked a second time, "What doest thou here, Elijah?" But like a broken record, Elijah repeated word for word his same sob story, "I, even only I, am left; and they seek my life, to take it away" (19:14).

Like Elijah, most of us today are running as fast as we can, trying to stay ahead of our fears. Elijah feared the sword. We fear the perils of falling behind, losing out, failing. So how did Elijah get back on the right track, and what can we learn from it?

First, God gave Elijah *direction*. "And the Lord God said unto him, Go, return on thy way to the wilderness of Damascus" (19:15). Second, the Lord gave Elijah a *task*. There were two kings and a prophet that needed anointing (19:16), so it was time to get cracking! Third, God gave his prophet *strength*, encouraging Elijah that he was not alone (19:18). On his own, Elijah's race ended in burn out and despair. Now, though Damascus was a long commute from Mount Horeb, he could make it.

Thirty Years on the Move

How much better if Elijah—if you and I—would quit our own rat races, come into God's presence, and hear his "still small voice."

Another Old Testament saint who needed an attitude adjustment was Jacob. For some thirty years he had been on the move, when God told him, "Arise, go up to Bethel and dwell there" (Genesis 35:1). Those thirty years had seen Jacob flee from the wrath of his brother Esau, had seen drama and deceit, marriage and children, then a return to his homeland and reconciliation with his brother.

Now Jacob faced a new crisis. Some of his sons wanted to inter-marry with the heathens against God's will; others did not. When a pagan prince was slain in the dispute, Jacob feared the heathen would "gather themselves together against me" (Genesis 34:30) and destroy his entire family. Though one of his daughters had already been defiled, Jacob was less worried about honor and more concerned for his own skin.

This was when, in the midst of the crisis, God told Jacob to "go up to Bethel." Why? Because it was the place where he had first met God. In Genesis 28 we read how, as Jacob fled from his brother, the Lord came to him in a dream. Jacob saw a ladder that reached from earth to heaven. God stood above it and declared that Jacob would be protected and would return home to found a great nation.

"And Jacob awaked out of his sleep, and he said, Surely the Lord is in this place ... [and] this is none but the house of God" (28:16-17). And that is what Bethel means, "House of God." That same day Jacob built a stone memorial and consecrated it with oil. Then he pledged his life to God and vowed to tithe all that he owned.

Back to Bethel

After thirty years on the move, and now facing his latest life crisis, Jacob would remember the significance of Bethel. He would remember how God had promised him, "And, behold, I am with thee and will keep thee in all places whither thou goest ... for I will not leave thee until I have done that which I have spoken to thee of" (28:15). He would remember how he had "vowed a vow, saying, If God will be with me ... then shall the Lord be my God" (28:20-21). And so the memory of his broken vow would remind Jacob of his own weakness and of God's faithfulness and strength.

And Jacob would not forget the altar he had built at Bethel. In the thirty years since then, the Bible does not record that he ever built another altar in his journeys. Perhaps this spiritual neglect is what brought Jacob to the end of his own way. So upon hearing God's command to go back to Bethel, he declared to all his family, "Put away the strange gods that are among you ... And let us arise, and go up to Bethel; and I will make an altar unto God" (Genesis 35:2-3).

The patriarch discovered anew that the Lord is faithful. His family forsook their idols "and they journeyed, and the terror of God was upon the cities that were round about them, and they did not pursue after the sons of Jacob" (35:4-5). Jacob's return to Bethel, to the house of God, did not mean the end of trials. Soon after their return, Jacob and his family suffered the loss of a beloved servant (35:8), while his dear wife Rachel died in childbirth (35:16-20). Nevertheless, in going back to the place where he first met God, Jacob gained the victory. For it was here that "God appeared unto Jacob again ... and blessed him" (35:9).

The Hardest Commute of All

Elijah never drove on an interstate, and Jacob never had to face a monster traffic jam. What do his examples mean for our mobile, restless, fast-paced suburban world today?

Let's go back to the admonition. "Let us run with patience the race that is set before us" (Hebrews 12:1). How do we run with patience. The verse continues and provides the answer. We run with patience by forsaking our own run-around and instead "looking unto Jesus the author and finisher of our faith" (12:2). And how can we be sure that Christ is able to see us through our course? Because in His work, He endured the longest and most difficult commute of all: "Who for the joy that was set before him endured the cross, despising the shame, and is set down at the right hand of the throne of God" (12:2).

Modern society doesn't slow down for the Christian. But Jesus offers direction, purpose, and strength to those who know and serve Him. And He offers something else the world cannot. "Come unto me, all ye that labour and are heavy laden, and I will give you rest" (Matthew 11:28). Rest for your soul when there's an accident on I-

95. Rest when there is construction on the interstate. Rest when you hit every stoplight on the way to mall.

How to claim it?

> *For we which have believed do enter into rest ... There remaineth therefore a rest to the people of God"* *(Hebrews 4:3,9)*

10.14.02

Fairfax County, Va. — The fatal shooting of an Arlington woman outside a Home Depot [Monday] night has been "conclusively linked" to the series of sniper shootings that have now resulted in nine deaths in the Washington area since Oct. 2 ... The victim of last night's attack was identified this morning as Linda Franklin, 47, of Arlington. She was an FBI analyst and the mother of two grown children ... She and her husband, Ted, were going to move to another home in the area on Friday and they were at the Home Depot buying supplies for the move and new house ...

For eighty-four agonizing hours, the Nation's Capital held its breath. It would not have seemed possible but, when the sniper killed again, the result was terror escalated to a whole new level. For the first time since the initial wave of shootings the gunman struck inside the Beltway, the psychological dividing line between the city's inner core and outer suburbs.

"At first I thought I was safe because it was only happening in Maryland," a nearby restaurant owner told *The Washington Post.* "Then there was a shooting in Virginia. So then I thought I was safe because it's too crowded in [our] little area. There's too much traffic and too many people. But now I have a totally different feeling." Another resident remarked, "I was surprised because before, you know, it was someplace else. I didn't think it would happen in Virginia. Then, when it came to Virginia, I thought, it's out there in Spotsylvania, it's rural ... not like here. Now I'm always looking over my shoulder and seeing white vans."

A semi-rural crossroads fifty years ago, the Seven Corners area stands astride the border of Arlington and Fairfax counties and the city of Falls Church, the very heart of urbanized Northern Virginia. Today the area is a highly developed residential and retail community served by four shopping centers, the largest being Seven Corners Shopping Center which houses more than a dozen national chains. The area is still a crossroads where no less than six roads converge—four local arteries and two major commuter highways, Route 50 and Route 7.

Just past 9 p.m. on Monday, October 14, Linda Franklin and her husband Ted completed their purchases at the Home Depot in Seven Corners Shopping Center. It was less than an hour before closing time, but the Arlington couple needed some items for their planned move into a new home. The two put their items into a shopping cart and walked over to their car, a two-seater red convertible that was parked on the ground level of a two-tier garage. The Franklins stood side by side, loading purchases into the trunk of the car, when at 9:15 a single gunshot struck Linda Franklin in the head. Ted Franklin jumped over and covered up his wife as she fell. But the 47-year-old FBI analyst, a breast cancer survivor who was looking forward to her first grandchild, had been instantly killed.

At the sound of the rifle, the shopping center was immediately convulsed in panic. "The whole world started running inside the store," said one witness who, upon hearing the shot, turned and saw the victim only a hundred yards away. Others reported that customers throughout the shopping center started weeping uncontrollably as news of the attack spread and stores were quickly locked and barred. A mother and her twin boys hunkered down in an adjacent bookstore, ultimately counting more than fifty police cars and two helicopters arriving out front.

Unlike the last four shootings which had occurred next to interstate highway ramps, at Seven Corners the gunman had no obvious or quick escape route. The area is a labyrinth of roads, side streets, and cul de sacs. To reach the nearest interstates, either I-66 or the Capital Beltway, the sniper would be forced to run a gauntlet of traffic lights in residential neighborhoods. The Home Depot itself is located just within Fairfax County, the most heavily populated jurisdiction in the Washington metropolitan area.

Given the lack of easy egress from Seven Corners, police could hope their "traffic lockdown" might at last catch the killer. Only a few days earlier, in response to the Prince William County slaying, Fairfax authorities had begun to activate an emergency operations center. According to a spokesman, the center was designed "so we could have units rapidly deployed anywhere and so we would have a central point to disseminate communications." This time, police shut down every road in the Seven Corners area and closed all major highways—including Interstates 66, 95, 395, and 495—within the entire Northern Virginia corridor. The Potomac River bridges leading into the District and Maryland were also closed. Vehicles were permitted to pass only in single file so they could be checked by officers carrying assault rifles. The action lasted for about three hours as backups of more than ten miles were reported.

Nevertheless, residents told local media that streets around Seven Corners remained open fifteen minutes after the attack, while Route 50 and I-66 were still flowing freely a half hour later. "Our traffic plan works best when we're dealing with a limited-access roadway, not urban streetscapes where there are dozens of routes of escape," said a Fairfax County police spokesman. Apparently the delay was enough as the sniper escaped a second area-wide dragnet.

Once again, frustrated authorities and residents were left to speculate on the meager evidence available. Excitement rose when a man stepped forward who claimed to have seen the killer, but his testimony turned out to be fabricated, perhaps in an attempt to collect reward money. Experts quoted in the media now took seriously a possible connection to Michaels Arts and Crafts since the chain has an outlet at Seven Corners Shopping Center. Others pointed out that, for the second week, no attacks occurred over the weekend. In both weeks, Friday shootings had been followed by Monday attacks.

At a press conference the day after the Seven Corners slaying, Fairfax County Police Chief J. Thomas Manger announced a "lookout" had been broadcast for a "light-colored" Chevy Astro van that had been seen leaving the area after the shooting. The vehicle had a silver ladder rack on the roof and its left tail light was not functioning, but information about its license plate number was lacking. Spotsylvania County Police also released new composite sketches of a Chevy Astro and a Ford Econo van, both white with a ladder rack on top, possibly seen after the previous killing in Massaponax.

Montgomery County Police Chief Charles Moose told reporters that Linda Franklin did not work at any FBI office concerned with the sniper investigation, and thus police discounted any link between her employment and the slaying. Then, answering questions about the prospect of getting a composite sketch of the killer, Moose replied that "if we have information that we feel needs to be in the public arena, would be helpful in the case, we will present that information ... You can feel the frustration, people want the picture."

People do want something tangible to help them grasp what is happening, observed James A. Fox, a professor of criminology and authority on serial killers. "The Boston Strangler, the Hillside Strangler, the Atlanta child murders, the Zodiac Killer, the coed murders at the University of Florida—none of them were like this. The risk here is not restricted by any demographic characteristic, so everyone feels like a target ... Here there is no pattern."

Chapter Six

The Parking Lot
and the Things We Value: Choices

Thirty-five years before a single .223-caliber bullet tragically took the life of Linda Franklin, my mother and I stood in the very same spot. Seven Corners Shopping Center was much smaller then. There was no parking garage, no Home Depot. There were no "big box" chain retailers then, not even any shopping malls.

If my mother and I could have picked up a newspaper from the future—if in 1967 we could have somehow read the awful news of October 14, 2002—we would not have understood its meaning. Not that crime or killing was unknown to us. A sniper had assassinated President Kennedy in 1963. And it would be a sniper who, in 1968, would gun down Dr. Martin Luther King, Jr.

No, the shocking brutality of murder was within our understanding. But we would not have understood why a killer would target Seven Corners Shopping Center.

Admittedly, we had Hecht's and Garfinkel's, two locally owned department stores. And Seven Corners had its share of local merchants. There was the optometrist, the shoe store, the candy shop. There was even a Woodward & Lothrop. But the parking lot was only crowded at Christmas. If a killer wanted to terrorize the Nation's Capital, there was nothing special about Seven Corners. It was simply our local shopping center.

What Used to Be

Seven Corners is a perfect microcosm of how our lives in suburbia have changed over the years. I know, because I lived there and watched it happen.

The simple shopping center of my childhood, filled with local merchants serving neighborhood customers, is no more. But traces of the area's past are still evident, if in name only. The Virginia suburb of Falls Church takes its name from an old church that once stood beside the falls of a country creek. In the Forties, Falls Church was still a semi-rural crossroads when its first radio station was built atop a garage that stood next to the veterinarian's office. Later, the postwar subdivision built at Seven Corners was called Sleepy Hollow, a name it still bears today. When the shopping center was built in the Fifties—with a department store, no less—local boosters believed that Seven Corners had come of age.

My family moved to the Seven Corners area in 1965. I was in second grade then and sometimes we bought my school clothes at Hecht's or Woodie's. Best of all, Seven Corners Shopping Center had the S&W Cafeteria. We didn't eat out very often—few families did back then—and so it was a special treat. Arlington Boulevard had not been widened and the Beltway was under construction. So the S&W was our only accessible choice for a family-priced night out. The McDonald's on Route 50 was also an option, with its red-and-white tiled interior and actual golden arches. But there was no indoor seating or drive-thru.

Those days were not destined to last. By the Seventies our McDonald's had lost its golden arches, and Seven Corners Shopping Center was failing. Huge retail complexes called "shopping malls" were being built in the outer suburbs, drawing away customers. They were actually enclosed and air-conditioned. Imagine that!

Seven Corners itself experimented briefly with becoming an enclosed shopping center. In time, however, the suburban malls became overbuilt and overcrowded. By the Nineties, customers started coming back to Falls Church. They were attracted by the convenient location—and by a new concept in retailing, the "destination" store. Owned by large national chains, with tens of thousands of square feet under a single roof, these superstores could buy in volume and outsell the local competition.

Choices and More Choices

When my mother and I were buying school clothes in the Sixties or eating at the S&W Cafeteria with the family, we would never have imagined what the Seven Corners area has become. In our day there was Seven Corners Shopping Center itself, a Zayre's store on Wilson Boulevard, a Lord & Taylor's on Leesburg Pike, plus a Ward's catalog store and the small Willston Shopping Center on Arlington Boulevard.

Thirty-five years later, when Linda Franklin was loading her car with purchases from Home Depot, she stood next to her husband Ted on the ground floor of a two-tier parking garage. In front of her was Arlington Boulevard, now widened into a major suburban commuter route. Across the road was yet another large shopping center, anchored by consumer electronics chain store. There was also the massively expanded Willston Shopping Center, which has taken over much of the parking lot of the now-closed Montgomery Ward's.

Behind Linda Franklin, in Seven Corners Shopping Center itself, was an array of chain stores—Shoppers Club, Barnes & Noble, Starbucks Coffee, Bath & Bodyworks, Payless Shoes, Off-Broadway Shoes, Ross Dress for Less, Dollar City, GNC Health Foods, Michaels Arts & Crafts, G Street Fabrics, Jo-Ann Fabrics—plus a Wendy's and a Pizzeria Uno in the parking lot.

The absence of any local merchants would have surprised us in 1967. How could a bookstore, a coffee shop, a fabric store, or a crafts store be part of a national chain? Even more amazing would have been the sheer growth in size, density, traffic and, most of all, the available choices. An entire store of nothing but bath products or health foods? Not one but two shoe stores, and discount stores at that? In my childhood, buying quality shoes was a fairly serious occasion. I even had my own shoe salesmen, just like I had a regular doctor. Mr. Tony, we called him. He fitted my shoes for me until I went to college. He eventually retired from that same store, before it was torn down for a retail-office complex.

A Single Shot

I miss the old Seven Corners. But if the truth be known, I have grown accustomed to all the choices that suburban life affords today. I am glad that discount shoes are available for my kids. And I am glad that Linda Franklin, a breast cancer survivor who was looking forward to her first grandchild, could buy a new home and furnish it through Home Depot. I would not turn back the clock to 1967.

But having so many choices, which seems to give our lives such freedom and autonomy, in a way creates increased dependence. What if our choices were taken from us? What if we had no choices—or just the choice between one thing and another? For twenty days the people of Washington faced an unprecedented situation. They feared for their lives and were forced to limit their activities. That too was part of the fear, as the ability to make normal daily choices was suddenly taken away.

The Bible has much to say about choices. Much of what it says, however, goes against the grain of our culture today. We are accustomed to having many choices. We expect stores to offer a wide selection of brands, features, and price ranges. If one store does not have what we want, then we go to another store in the next shopping center.

Chances are Mr. Tony might not last long in our world today. When it comes to kid's shoes, most of us would rather have lots of choices than pay a little bit more for personal service. For the same reason, the discount chain probably would not pay Mr. Tony enough salary to keep him as a career employee. Then too, Mr. Tony went home to his family at the end of the day. When I was a boy growing up near Seven Corners, the idea of "24/7" would have seemed like overkill. Today, the thought of a store not being open on *our* schedule makes us frustrated. The few times we find there is "nothing open" makes us angry and we cannot deal with it.

Even banker's hours are a relic of the past. Banks today provide walk-up and drive-thru service from eight to five, and offer ATM service around the clock. Furthermore, we expect stores not only to have *what* we want *when* we want it, but to be located *where* we can enjoy convenient road access and ample parking. Customer surveys consistently show that convenience and location are the major factors that drive consumer purchasing decisions.

Neither are we willing to wait in exercising our choices. Thirty-five years ago, if my parents wanted to buy one of those new color TV sets, they waited until enough money was saved up and then paid cash. Today we tell ourselves, "Why wait so long, when I could be enjoying that home entertainment system now?" After all, credit is easy. Credit card companies no longer even require us to fill out applications. So we expect stores to sell us their wares on credit, even as we pay off one credit card by borrowing against another. When the occasional Chinese carry-out does not take credit, we hardly know what to do.

When Few Are Chosen

In such a world where choices are the rule, where the customer truly is king, what chance does Jesus stand? He said, "No man cometh to the Father, but by Me" (John 14:6). He demands, "If any man will come after me, let him deny himself, and take up his cross daily, and follow me" (Luke 9:23). That does not leave much room for choice. The spirit of our age nods in agreement with the idea that God is "not willing that any should perish" (2 Peter 3:9), but we rebel at Christ's declaration, "For many are called, but few are chosen" (Matthew 22:14).

The world of my boyhood days had its problems. Racism, war, assassinations, riots, political scandals, superpower conflict. I watched my parents pack our suitcases during the Cuban Missile Crisis. I sat on my father's shoulders, overlooking Memorial Bridge and watching the funeral procession of President Kennedy. My tenth birthday party was canceled—we had tickets to see the Washington Senators on opening day—when Martin Luther King Jr. was assassinated and riots set Washington aflame. When I was sixteen and a page in the House of Representatives I witnessed the Watergate hearings and learned that my President had lied to me.

Yet in the world of my childhood, kids wore dress clothes to school and did not address grown-ups by their first names. Adults accepted constraints too. If stores were closed at night and on Sundays, people somehow got by. We did not have as may choices as suburban Americans have today. But in the culture of that era, neither did we have as much trouble accommodating ourselves to authority and accepting constraints on our choices.

An Unattractive Gospel?

What then do we make of Jesus Christ—and His exclusive claims—in our world today? The spirit of our times is much more in tune with the idea that "all roads lead to Heaven." If my religion works for me, fine. But how dare I claim to have a monopoly on the truth or force my religion on another person. After all, he has a right to make his own choices, and those choices are as valid as mine.

A gospel that restricts men's lives and narrows their choices, that imposes on them a straightjacket of do's and don'ts, is an unattractive gospel indeed. But is that the gospel that Jesus offers us today?

There is no way around it. In God's economy the choice is between heaven or hell, salvation in Christ or damnation without Him. "Neither is there salvation in any other: for there is none other name under heaven given among men, whereby we must be saved" (Acts 4:12). The choice cannot be any more clear than that. God is perfect and cannot admit anything less into His presence. And because He is perfectly holy and just, God must punish sin. "For the wages of sin is death" (Romans 6:23).

Yet you and I certainly are *not* perfect! "For all have sinned, and come short of the glory of God" (Romans 3:23). Do we then have no hope? The good news is that Jesus Christ has already paid for our sins, has covered them with His blood, through his death on the cross. "But the gift of God is eternal life through Jesus Christ our Lord" (Romans 6:23) to all who, in faith, place their trust in Him as Savior. "That if thou shalt confess with thy mouth the Lord Jesus, and shalt believe in thine heart that God hath raised him from the dead, thou shalt be saved" (Romans 10:9).

But since we live in a world accustomed to choices, we can also look at the issue from a "pro-choice" point of view. Yes, it is true that God offers only one choice that leads to salvation. "Enter ye in at the strait gate: for wide is the gate, and broad is the way, that leadeth to destruction, and many there be which go in thereat: because strait is the gate, and narrow is the way, which leadeth unto life, and few there be that find it" (Matthew 7:13-14). And yet, is it not the act of a loving God to provide only *one* choice, a choice that is simple and easy to understand?

Too Much of a Good Thing

What if, instead of one way, there were hundreds or thousands of ways to salvation? That each way was different and God let us choose? In that case, we would be confused and constantly worried about whether or not we had made a choice that God approved. With so many divergent and seemingly conflicting choices, it would be easy for wrong choices to seem like right ones. How would we know the difference? We would never be able to tell!

Or just as likely, if there were thousands of choices that led to heaven—and God let us choose—we would come to believe that the choosing was based on our own cleverness. We would not thank God for *allowing* us to choose our own way, but insist to Him that choosing was our *right*. Rather than acknowledging His sovereignty, we would demand God accept our choices.

After all, that is the way we view our expectation of consumer choices today, that it is a right. But in light of the sniper attacks, consider this. Suppose God permitted us to choose our own way to heaven. And suppose some difficult circumstance came along—accidents, illnesses, finances—that restricted or eliminated our ability to choose? We would feel insecure and fearful. Far better that the issue of heaven or hell is not up to us, but to a God who "is able to deliver us" (Daniel 3:17).

As a guy I admit that I do not like shopping. But if there was a "Seven Corners of the soul" and I had to make the one choice on which my eternal destiny depended, then I would not want to shop around and wonder what choice was best. I would rather know exactly what I needed, walk straight into the one store that carried it, and go directly to the item I required. In other words, I am glad to know that I need a Savior and I can go straight to Jesus without having to wonder about my choice.

Limits or Liberty?

In the awful aftermath of the sniper attacks, there is one other lesson we can learn about making choices. Seven Corners was once a rural community. Farmers there had fewer choices but, being able to supply their own needs, enjoyed more independence. As modern American suburbanites, we have the seeming freedom of endless choices. But we are dependent on others to stock the products we want, be located and open according to our convenience, and extend us credit so that we need not defer our desires. If we are somehow cut off from these things, as we were for the twenty awful days of the sniper shootings, then we are paralyzed.

The same idea applies to our spiritual lives. Many people believe that "being a Christian" restricts a person's choices and freedoms. The Bible says not to lie, cheat, steal or murder (okay, we agree on that), and to forego drinking and partying and sex outside of marriage (now, that may be a bit intolerant).

But the fact is that trusting Christ leads to *more* freedom and not less. "When we were children, [we] were in bondage under the elements of the world" (Galatians 4:3), for while the unrighteous "promise liberty, they themselves are the servants of corruption: for of whom a man is overcome, of the same is he brought in bondage" (2 Peter 2:19). How much better to "be delivered from the bondage of corruption into the glorious liberty of the children of God" (Romans 8:21) and to "stand fast therefore in the liberty wherewith Christ hath made us free, and be not entangled again with the yoke of bondage" (Galatians 5:1). That is why Jesus declared to those who place their trust in Him, "And ye shall know the truth, and the truth shall make you free" (John 8:32).

The Christian is told to live "as free, and not using your liberty for a cloak of maliciousness, but as the servants of God" (2 Peter 2:16). If you give your life to Christ, you are only constrained from using your freedom to make evil choices. But you are entirely free to choose all good things, for "every good gift and every perfect gift is from above, and cometh down from the Father of lights" (James

1:17). As a Christian, you have more choices than ever, for you are now the child of a God who "shall supply all your need according to his riches in glory by Christ Jesus" (Philippians 4:19).

That is why "every one that asketh receiveth," for compared even to wicked men who "know how to give good gifts unto your children, how much more shall your Father which is in heaven give good things to them that ask him?" (Matthew 7:8,11). Place your trust in Christ and then "delight thyself also in the Lord," for when your choices are the same as His, then "he shall give thee the desires of thine heart" (Psalm 37:4).

The Washington of my youth is gone forever. After 9/11 and now the D.C. Sniper shootings, my hometown today will no longer be the same as it was. But amidst all the changes that we are experiencing today, one choice will never be taken from us. "I have set before you life and death, blessing and cursing: therefore choose life" (Deuteronomy 30:19).

How may that life be chosen?

> *And this is the record, that God hath given to us eternal life, and this life is in his Son. He that hath the Son hath life"* (1 John 5:11-12)

10.19.02

Ashland, Va. — A 37-year-old man was shot [Saturday] night outside a restaurant near Interstate 95, north of Richmond, in an attack that appeared similar to the sniper shootings that have spread fear across the Washington region. Like 11 attacks attributed to the elusive gunman since Oct. 2, last night's shooting drew a massive police response in which officers combed the immediate area around the shooting site in Ashland, Va., and stopped and scrutinized vehicles on major roads from Richmond to Washington ... The shooting victim was described as a man from outside Virginia who was traveling through the area and had stopped to get food and gasoline ...

On October 19, 2002, the D.C. Sniper struck for the first time on a Saturday. And for the second time, the gunmen left a handwritten message at the scene. But unlike the taunting five-word scrawl written on a tarot card at the October 7 shooting in Bowie, this time the killer provided a detailed three-page letter—and gave the case a bizarre new twist.

Just before eight on that Saturday night, near an I-95 ramp about eighty miles south of the Seven Corners shooting, a husband and wife paid for their dinner at the Ponderosa Steakhouse. The couple (identity withheld) were travelers from Melbourne, Florida, who had stopped for gas and food at the exit in Ashland, Virginia. As the two emerged from the restaurant at 7:59 p.m., the man was hit in the abdomen by a bullet from a high-powered rifle. He took three steps and then collapsed. Bystanders attempted to stop his bleeding until help could arrive. The man was rushed to the Medical College of Virginia hospital in Richmond, where surgeons ultimately saved his life.

Again the sniper had returned to the all-too-familiar pattern of attacking near an interstate ramp. Ashland is popular with travelers for its easy on-off access, multiple choices for gasoline and fast food, and as the last stop before the Richmond I-295 interchange and metro area. Police responded by closing Interstate 95 as far south as Henrico County, just north of Richmond. But the gunman's escape was aided by quick egress and by surprise. The Ponderosa, located on Route 54, is only a quarter-mile from both I-95 to the east and Route 1 which parallels the interstate on the west. And Ashland was not viewed as a likely target since it is not considered part of the Washington area.

Then, in a strange turn of events, that same night the sniper apparently called a tip line. A letter, he told investigators, had been left at the scene tacked to a tree and wrapped in plastic. Authorities found the letter at the place indicated, a letter that was addressed

For you Mr Police
"Call me God"

The handwritten letter warned authorities, "Do not release to the press," and then expressed frustration over official "incompetence" at disregarding eight phone calls—all detailed—as a "hoax or joke." Because these attempts to "start negotiation" had been ignored, the sniper wrote, "your failure to respond has cost you five lives."

The sniper then issued a ransom demand, directing authorities to place ten million dollars into a Visa account—which investigators then traced to an ATM card reported stolen on the West Coast and used illicitly in Tacoma, Washington. "We will have unlimited withdrawal at any atm [sic] worldwide," he further demanded.

According to the letter, the sniper would contact authorities at 6 a.m. the following morning by calling the number of a Ponderosa restaurant in Virginia. Authorities would then have until 9 a.m. Monday to comply with the ransom instructions. Then the killer issued a taunting challenge:

Try to catch us [while] withdrawing [money], at least you
will have less body bags, but if trying to catch us now

*[without paying the ransom is] more important then pre-
pare you[r] body bags. If we give you our word that is what
takes place. "Word is Bond." P.S. Your children are not safe
anywhere at any time.*

The next morning, a Sunday, authorities missed the sniper's
phone call due to a problem with the number provided in the letter. What ensued is one of the most unusual episodes in the
annals of American crime as Montgomery County Police Chief
Charles Moose, head of the joint task force, attempted to communicate with the sniper through the national media:

Sunday, October 20, 7:10 p.m. Chief Moose faced the press
and makes a plea to the killer, "To the person who left us a message at the Ponderosa [Saturday] night, you gave us a telephone
number. Call us at the phone number you provided."

Monday, October 21, 8:30 a.m. Police received a call from a
person believed to be the sniper. The call is traced to the vicinity
of an Exxon station in the Richmond area, where police discover
a white Plymouth Voyager minivan with a luggage rack that is
parked next to a public phone. Two men are apprehended but
subsequently cleared. Meanwhile, authorities have difficulty
understanding the call itself, which they say was a partially unin-
telligible tape-recorded message played into the phone.

Monday, October 21, 10 a.m. Again, Chief Moose went before
the cameras and publicly acknowledged the phone call had been
received. "We are going to respond to a message that we have
received," he states. "We will respond later. We are preparing
that response at this time."

Monday, October 21, 4:15 p.m. Analysis of the morning phone
call failed to retrieve the full message. Using the media to again
carry his message to the sniper he said, "The person you called
could not understand everything you said. The audio was unclear
and we want to get it right. Call us back so that we can clearly
understand."

Before dawn the next day, Tuesday, October 22, the sniper
answered—leaving another letter at the scene of another shooting.

Chapter Seven

The Restaurant
and the Things We Value: Leisure

I n recent years I have come to know the Ashland Exit very well.
Now that I live further south in another state, Ashland is the best
place on I-95 to stop for gas and food after visiting family in D.C.
Ashland is the last exit before the I-295 interchange and the Richmond
metro area. And with several gas stations, fastfood chains and a Ponderosa Steakhouse, plus easy on-off access to the interstate, the Ashland
Exit is the logical choice.

Just like in Washington, suburban growth in Richmond—capital of
Virginia and among the hundred largest cities in America—follows
the interstates. So in addition to visitors, the Ponderosa Steakhouse
also attracts its share of locals. Ashland is a growing town in its own
right, with historic Randolph-Macon College and the popular King's
Dominion theme park located nearby. Ashland even has two Christian radio stations.

Also like in Washington, and nearly everywhere else in America, a
place to eat out is important to people in Ashland. Residents there
also have home entertainment centers, cable and satellite television,
and high-speed broadband Internet access—not to mention the two
Christian radio stations. They have RVs for camping in the Blue
Ridge Mountains and boats for fishing on the Chesapeake Bay. They
join health clubs and buy time shares and, in short, pursue leisure
and recreation just like the rest of us.

Entertainment, c. 1967

Now rewind to 1967. Once again I am a third-grader in the Boulevard Manor subdivision of Arlington, just east of Seven Corners off
Wilson Boulevard and Route 50. I have two younger sisters, my
mother stays at home, and my father has a good job as a government contractor.

What did we do for leisure and entertainment?

Well, we ate at the S&W Cafeteria in Seven Corners Shopping Center about two or three times a year. And maybe once a year, for a birthday or anniversary, mom and dad would get a babysitter and go to the *La Boheme* at Willston Shopping Center. But that was about it. My dad, like most dads in 1967, put a high priority on family meals at home. "There should be at least one time during the day when we all get together and talk to each other," he would say. After all, my mother did not have a microwave oven in 1967—or a dishwasher. There were no pre-cooked convenience foods as we know them today, just the occasional "TV dinner." So if my mother was going to spend hours preparing dinner and dessert from scratch—and more time to wash dishes afterward—then the whole family had better come running as soon as she called!

If we had free time in the evening, then our main entertainment choices were four TV channels, a board game, reading the paper, or playing the piano. Since mom stayed at home and shopped during the day, we did not have to go out at night to run errands. Every Sunday we went to my father's parents for dinner, followed by a time of family conversation or listening together to the hi-fi. Afterward, we watched *The Wonderful World of Disney* on my grandparents' color TV set, then played Scrabble or cribbage until it was time to go home. Grandma and Grandpa would also take us for occasional drives in the country, to teach us about Virginia history.

Of course, not every evening was free. There was football or baseball practice, Cub Scout and PTA meetings. Mom went to bridge club once a month, and we also joined the community pool. For our government contracting business, my grandfather got season tickets for the Senators and Redskins and sometimes let dad and me use them. That summer for a vacation we rented a cabin at a state park on the Potomac River near the Chesapeake Bay. In the years to follow, when my mother's parents retired to Florida, we would visit them for a vacation every other summer. Since Disney World was not built until 1976, the closest we came to a theme park was Cypress Gardens or Weeki Wachee Springs.

My personal pastimes were equally quaint by today's standards. I read books voraciously, actually enjoyed practicing the piano, collected electric slot cars and track, rode my bike all over the neighborhood, and had the great good fortune of living behind the county ballfields for pickup games every day after school.

Channels and Choices

This is what a white-collar Washington suburban family did for fun
in 1967. Supper at home. Four TV channels. Reading the paper. Cub
Scouts and PTA, bridge club and community pool. Ball practice.
Visiting family every Sunday. Vacationing with my grandparents.

Now fast forward to today.

I think you can fill in the picture. Family meals and dinnertime
conversations are mostly a lost art. In the suburbs of today, eating
out is not just two or three times a year, but two or three a week—
or a day! Americans now drink more soda than water, and many eat
out more than at home.

Entertainment? Evening newspapers are extinct. And instead of
just four TV channels we have access, by cable or satellite, to hundreds—news channels, sports channels, movie channels, shopping
channels, fashion channels, travel channels, food channels, home and
garden channels, women's channels, children's channels, family channels. The notion of a "home entertainment center" would have
been unthinkable when I was a boy. We actually had to get up if we
wanted to change channels or adjust the vertical control, and we
needed room on top of the TV set to adjust the antenna. Today we
have wide-screen TVs and portable TVs, flat-screen TVs and digital
TVs. Of course, record players have long since given way to CD
players and now MP3 players. And even videos are being phased out
for DVDs.

Of course, the content of our entertainment has also changed. As
a small child who slept very little, I remember that TV stations did
not broadcast twenty-four hours a day back then. I used to watch
the national anthem at midnight, then wake up in the morning and
see the test-pattern while waiting for my favorite shows—like "Cap-
tain Kangaroo" or "Kukla, Fran and Ollie." Washington also had its
share of local kids' TV shows. There was Ranger Hal, Cousin Cup-
cake, and "Romper Room" with Miss Shirley.

Adult fare was also tame by modern standards. Instead of reality
shows, we watched variety shows with hosts such as Ed Sullivan,
Jackie Gleason, Red Skelton, Perry Como, Andy Williams, and Carol
Burnett. And sitcoms like "Father Knows Best" and "Leave It to
Beaver" may have been idealized but, unlike today's fare, the shows
were clean—and had great theme songs! ("A horse is a horse, of
course, of course ...")

Washington, my hometown, was even the setting for a sitcom of its own. Each week Maxwell Smart and his lovely sidekick "99" led the fearless agents of C.O.N.T.R.O.L. against the evil schemes of C.H.A.O.S. And while the "Cone of Silence" has never caught on, whenever I see someone make a cell call I always think of Agent 86 and his amazing "shoe phone."

Then there is the computer. When dad would let me visit his office in downtown Washington, I loved to play with the latest gadgets—the Dictaphone and even the Address-O-Graph. By the time I went to college, however, high technology was on the march. I registered for classes with IBM punchcards, played Pong on my Atari, and wrote class papers on my own electric typewriter. A few years after graduation I was thrilled to get a Selectric with a built-in correcting ribbon. That year I even bought my first VCR. By the late Eighties, I got a PC at work and one at home to do my writing. At the time, I saved my manuscripts on 5¼-inch floppy disks and mailed them to my editors. Then Federal Express invented overnight delivery—then everybody got fax machines—and now I just attach my manuscripts to an e-mail. Wow!

With the Internet today I can send e-mail, do research for my writing and even buy new books online, all without leaving home. For entertainment I can bookmark my favorite websites—like the one, ironically, that features audio streaming of old-time radio shows. And I can read *The Washington Post* every day—in fact, several times a day when the Redskins are playing!

The Telephone Rings

To me, however, one story about today's leisure and entertainment culture sums it all up. Let me tell you about it.

Donna and I are sitting at home eating dinner when the phone rings. We both frown for a moment, then Donna volunteers to pick it up.

"Hi, this is Derek with the Leisure Travel Club ..."

You know the rest of the spiel. But they're offering a fifty-dollar gift certificate at Red Lobster if we come to their sales center and listen to a presentation. Our anniversary is coming up and, since Donna likes seafood, she asks me to go. We both dread these presentations, but how could I say no?

At the appointed day and time, we get into our car and head down to the Leisure Travel Club sales office. Inside is a room full of small tables where sales reps are talking to seemingly eager couples. Donna and I go to the reception desk, fill out the "Leisure Travel Club Vacation Survey," and then are introduced to Chuck.

Chuck sits us down at one of the tables, looks over our survery form, and expresses surprise that we spend so little each year on a vacation.

"Donna, you can not let Mark work too hard," he laughs. "You gotta get him to take a break." Then turning a bit more serious, Chuck tells us in a manner of friendly concern, "You know, it's not healthy to just work all the time without a real break. And it's not good for your family, either."

Not quite an accurate characterization. But in the interests of getting this over with, I hold my tongue. Since we are not biting, Chuck tries a different tactic. Divide and conquer! He asks Donna that, if money were no object and she could travel anywhere, then where would she go?

"Well, I've always wanted to go to England."

Of course, that leads to a discussion of how the Leisure Travel Club can get us there. By now, Donna is getting impatient and wants to know hard numbers. Since nothing else has worked, Chuck puts on his reading glasses and pulls out his sales presentation notebook. Page by page, he builds his case. Testimonials. Charts and graphs. All very logical.

"Now, with the rising costs of vacation travel," Chuck concludes, "wouldn't you like to lock in today's prices for the rest of your life? And under our plan, you can budget your travel dollars by paying a set amount every month ..."

Just what I need, another fixed monthly expense. I can see paying my electric bill through monthly averaging. But my vacations? Leisure is a "fixed" cost, right up there with my house payments and grocery bills? Sorry, but to my mind a vacation is still an extra— along with going to restaurants, ordering pizzas, subscribing to premium channels, getting tickets to the game, and buying CDs.

Yet even Christian money management seminars I have attended advise churchgoers to budget their leisure and entertainment expenses. Their advice is not wrong. It is simply a recognition that even Christians today spend a lot of money, more than we often realize, on fastfood and eating out and all those "extras" we now expect in our suburban lifestyles.

Rest and Refreshment

Now, Chuck was right to an extent. God does intend for His people to get the rest they need. The Lord Himself rested after His work of creation, but not because He was tired! "It is a sign between me and the children of Israel for ever: for in six days the Lord made heaven and earth, and on the seventh day He rested, and was refreshed" (Exodus 31:17). He laid down the example that labor must be followed by periodic rest for the human body to operate at peak efficiency.

Think of your life for a moment as a speech. A good speech is not just sound and words. An accomplished orator also uses pauses to gain attention, drive his points home, and prepare the audience for his climax. In the same way, the span of human life is more effective when punctuated by activity and rest.

"Six days thou shalt do thy work, and on the seventh day thou shalt rest: that thine ox and thine ass may rest, and the son of thy handmaid, and the stranger, may be refreshed" (Exodus 23:12). *Rest* is the primary emphasis of the original creation decree for a sabbath day, a regular time for physical rejuvenation and refreshment. "See, for that the Lord hath given you the sabbath, therefore he giveth you on the sixth day the bread of two days; abide ye every man in his place, let no man go out of his place on the seventh day" (Exodus 16:29).

Scripture also shows how God was concerned for the refreshment of the land and the nation. The "Sabbatical Year" allowed farmers to leave their land fallow every seventh year so the soil could rejuvenate itself. Likewise, the "Year of Jubilee" ensured that no one in Israel was permanently impoverished. Every fiftieth year (that is, after every seven sevens of years) all land would revert to the original family owners so that real property was leased rather than sold.

So powerful is the concept of rest, in the New Testament it becomes an illustration of personal salvation. "There remaineth a rest to the people of God, for he that is entered into his rest, he also hath ceased from his own works, as God did from His" (Hebrews 4:9-10). And those who "repent ye therefore, and be converted, that your sins may be blotted out" can then look forward to "when the times of refreshing shall come from the presence of the Lord" (Acts 3:19).

Jesus Himself knew the importance of physical rest. The urgency of His earthly task was so great that "I must work the works of Him that sent me while it is day" (John 9:4). But the Lord also sought refreshment by "departing into a solitary place" and advising His disciples to "come ye apart and rest a while" (Mark 1:35, 6:31).

Changes in the Workplace

Our modern pursuit of leisure, recreation, and entertainment often goes far beyond simple rest and refreshment. Actually, it can be a part of our striving for self-expression and self-fulfillment. Now, there is nothing innately wrong with expression and fulfillment. But the degree to which we pursue it must be balanced. In fact, the Bible has much to say about the balance between work and play. Few subjects are more relevant for our lives in the suburbs.

During my years in Washington, I witnessed a fundamental change in the relationship between employers and employees. My mother's father, as well as my father-in-law, both spent some thirty years of their careers working for the same government agency. One was a civilian machinist for the Navy Department and the other a draftsman for the Veterans Administration. Both retired with pensions and official certificates of commendation.

Today, few employees retire after thirty or forty years of service with the same employer. Most people today cannot imagine staying that long in the same job and instead change positions every three to five years. The old idea of giving lifetime service to a company in exchange for lifetime job security is nearly gone. After a generation of corporate downsizing, few companies are willing or able to commit themselves to their employees for an entire career.

Given the change in employers, it is not surprising that employees have changed too. Accustomed to job mobility, most Americans would feel stifled by the expectation to spend their entire working lives with the same company. In my writing for business journals I have often spoken with career consultants, and the advice they give to white-collar professionals today goes something like this:

Do not expect to be with the same company five years from now. Companies today talk about loyalty, but the bottom-line comes first. Do not think that you're going to work for a company the rest of your career. That is not realistic. Instead, think of yourself as your being your own company, "John Smith Inc." You have to sell yourself, market yourself, promote yourself—then hire yourself out to the company that best meets your needs and goals. If your company no longer meets your needs, move on to a company that will. After all, if you stopped being needed by your company, they wouldn't hesitate to let you go. Of course, when you work for a company do the very best job you can. But in today's economy, you have to look out for yourself—because no employer is going to do that for you.

That advice reflects the reality of the workplace today. For my part, I would not turn back the clock to the days of paternal Big Business. Being expected to work your whole career for the same company had disadvantages too. But I think something has been lost in our professional world, the idea of working for something bigger than ourselves.

So we have a nation of people who suffer through the week and live for the weekend. Most pursue leisure and entertainment, in part because they find no transcendent satisfaction through our work. We have already addressed how God recognizes our need for rest and refreshment. What can the Bible can teach us about work?

A Bible Story

During the years I worked in Washington, it was my habit to keep a Bible on my desk. Other co-workers kept the latest bestsellers about career success or pop psychology on their desks. So I felt entitled to my own preference.

How three different bosses handled the matter was very interesting. One boss quietly came into my office each night and put my Bible on the shelf, so I would take the hint to keep it off my desk. Another boss called me into her office, yelled that a Bible was "totally inappropriate," and fired me after a month. The third boss came by my office one day and, with a tone of friendly concern, told me, "If I were you, I would think about whether or not I was projecting a professional image."

How sad that the Bible is considered "unprofessional" today. Even in my father's day, employees who were moral and God-fearing, who went to church and practiced the Bible, were considered assets to a company. They were the kind of employees that bosses looked for. But as I discovered, times have changed.

The point my bosses tried to make was that religion belonged in my personal life and not in the workplace, that the two spheres should be kept separate. However, in the Bible we learn that such "compartmentalization" is not possible for the Christian. All aspects of their lives and work belong to God. In fact, the Bible teaches that our workplace relationships are vitally important to maintaining a good Christian testimony.

Executive Summaries

At least four New Testament passages—Ephesians 6, Colossians 3-4, 1 Timothy 5-6, and Titus 2—portray our conduct at work as part of our overall conduct and testimony as Christians. All four passages give a broad survey of God's desire for the various relationships in our lives—as spouses, parents, children, elder or younger. And all four include the employer-employee relationship.

In other words, my professional life cannot be separated from my life as a whole. And just what do these passages actually teach about our conduct at work?

> *Servants, be obedient to them that are your masters according to the flesh, with fear and trembling, in singleness of your heart, as unto Christ; not with eyeservice, as menpleasers; but as the servants of Christ, doing the will of God from the heart; with good will doing service, as to the Lord, and not to men: knowing that whatsoever good thing any man doeth, the same shall he receive of the Lord, whether he be bond or free. And, ye masters, do the same things unto them, forbearing threatening: knowing that your Master also is in heaven; neither is there respect of persons with him. (Ephesians 6:5-9)*

Executive Summary: Do your work with a whole heart, even when no one is watching. You are really doing this work as a Christian serving God, from Whom is your reward. Bosses, the same applies to you. God is also watching you and, when it comes to rewards, He does not care whether you are a janitor or a CEO.

> *Servants, obey in all things your masters according to the flesh; not with eyeservice, as menpleasers; but in singleness of heart, fearing God; and whatsoever ye do, do it heartily, as to the Lord, and not unto men; knowing that of the Lord ye shall receive the reward of the inheritance: for ye serve the Lord Christ. But he that doeth wrong shall receive for the wrong which he hath done: and there is no respect of persons. Masters, give unto your servants that which is just and equal; knowing that ye also have a Master in heaven. (Col 3:22-4:1)*

Executive Summary: Ditto, memo above.

> *Let as many servants as are under the yoke count their own masters worthy of all honour, that the name of God and his doctrine be not blasphemed. And they that have believing masters, let them not despise them, because they are brethren; but rather do them service, because*

they are faithful and beloved, partakers of the benefit. These things teach and exhort. (1 Tim 6:1-2)

Executive Summary: Employees, respect your bosses. Otherwise you will give the enemy cause to reproach your God. And if your boss is a Christian, do not use that as an excuse to slack off and expect him to cut you a break.

Exhort servants to be obedient unto their own masters, and to please them well in all things; not answering again; not purloining, but shewing all good fidelity; that they may adorn the doctrine of God our Saviour in all things. (Titus 2:9-10)

Executive Summary: At work you must be obedient and service-minded, not back-talking or stealing. You must be loyal to your employer. This is a good Christian testimony.

Lesson From a Master

When I was still a young man in my career, a boss gave me a lesson for which I have ever been grateful, one that changed my whole perspective. He had retired from the military as a chief master sergeant, and I appreciated his quiet fairness. One day he called me into his office and asked me if I had done a task he had requested the previous day via memo.

"No, sir," I replied. "I've had some other projects I was working on that I needed to do first."

The old master sergeant looked me straight in the eye. Then with a quiet voice that conveyed both firmness and kindness to a young subordinate, he answered, "Now, do not you think if it was important enough for me to ask it, then it should be important enough for you to do it?"

For me, that is the essence of the biblical work ethic. As someone who has fussed and fumed at licking my share of envelopes, I have found doing work "as unto the Lord" infuses even the most menial task with an eternal purpose. The Lord wants me to "please them [my bosses] well in all things" and tells me that, in so doing, I thereby "adorn the doctrine of our God the Savior in all things."

For that reason, "Whatsoever thy hand findeth to do, do it with thy might" (Ecclesiastes 9:10). And our work serves other important eternal purposes. By it, a man "shall bear his own burden" (Galatians 6:5) and not be a burden to others; indeed, he can "labour, working with his hands the thing which is good, that he may have to give to him that needeth" (Ephesians 4:28). By contrast, "if any provide not for his own, and specially for those of his own house, he hath denied the faith" and invited reproach upon his God (1 Timothy 5:8)

Finally, God wants us to work for our own good. "If any would not work, neither should he eat. For we hear that there are some which walk among you disorderly, working not at all, but are busybodies. Now them that are such we command and exhort by our Lord Jesus Christ, that with quietness they work, and eat their own bread" (2 Thessalonians 3:10-12). Labor is not only a means to avoid poverty, but to avoid idleness that leads to sin.

By approaching our work as a vital part of our life and service to God—by not "compartmentalizing" our personal and professional lives—we can derive great satisfaction from our labor. This is God's intention, that "thou shalt eat the labour of thine hands: happy shalt thou be, and it shall be well with thee" (Psalm 128:2). The joy is not in meeting the needs of the body, but in living out our love for God through the work He has given us to do. In this way, "every man should eat and drink, and enjoy the good of all his labour, it is the gift of God" (Ecclesiates 3:13).

Finding No Satisfaction

Many people today view work as simply a means to afford their leisure and entertainment. There is a man in the Bible who did that. As a king he could afford every pleasure that life could offer. And he wrote about his experience of using work only as a way to buy the "fun" that he desired.

> I said in mine heart, Go to now, I will prove thee with mirth, therefore enjoy pleasure ... I made me great works; I builded me houses; I planted me vineyards: I made me gardens and orchards, and I planted trees in them of all kind of fruits: I made me pools of water, to water therewith the wood that bringeth forth trees ... I gathered me also silver and gold ...

> I gat me men singers and women singers, and the delights of the sons of men, as musical instruments, and that of all sorts. So I was great, and increased more than all that were before me ... And whatsoever mine eyes desired I kept not from them, I withheld not my heart from any joy; for my heart rejoiced in all my labour: and this was my portion of all my labour.

> *Then I looked on all the works that my hands had wrought, and on the labour that I had laboured to do: and, behold, all was vanity and vexation of spirit, and there was no profit under the sun ... Then said I in my heart, As it happeneth to the fool, so it happeneth even to me ... seeing that which now is in the days to come shall all be forgotten ...*
>
> *Therefore I hated life; because the work that is wrought under the sun is grievous unto me: for all is vanity and vexation of spirit. Yea, I hated all my labour which I had taken under the sun: because I should leave it unto the man that shall be after me ... Therefore I went about to cause my heart to despair of all the labour which I took under the sun.*
>
> *For there is a man whose labour is in wisdom, and in knowledge, and in equity; yet to a man that hath not laboured therein shall he leave it for his portion. This also is vanity and a great evil ... For all his days are sorrows, and his travail grief; yea, his heart taketh not rest in the night. This is also vanity.*
>
> *There is nothing better for a man, than that he should eat and drink, and that he should make his soul enjoy good in his labour. This also I saw, that it was from the hand of God ... For God giveth to a man that is good in his sight wisdom, and knowledge, and joy: but to the sinner he giveth travail, to gather and to heap up, that he may give to him that is good before God. This also is vanity and vexation of spirit. (Ecclesiastes 2)*

The man who wrote these words was Solomon. He did not have to deal with a long commute, but his story is lived out by millions who labor each day in Washington and in cities and suburbs everywhere in America. Solomon tried the advice of that old TV commercial, the one that proclaimed, "It doesn't get any better than this!" But Solomon learned that such advice did not work. Laboring only to afford his pleasures proved to be empty and vain. Only laboring for God can bring satisfaction both to our work and our leisure.

A Good Future

There is another reason for the Christian to do heartily the work God has set before him. While those who in life rejected Christ sare judged to damnation, those who believed are judged as to their rewards.

> *Every man's work shall be made manifest: for the day shall declare it, because it shall be revealed by fire; and the fire shall try every man's*

work of what sort it is. If any man's work abide which he hath built thereupon, he shall receive a reward. If any man's work shall be burned, he shall suffer loss: but he himself shall be saved; yet so as by fire" (1 Corinthians 3:13-15)

What is your work accomplishing for eternity? Whether you are a CEO or a data entry clerk, whether you work in an office or a cubicle—whatever you do, you can serve out God's purpose for your life, "knowing that of the Lord ye shall receive the reward of the inheritance: for ye serve the Lord Christ ... and there is no respect of persons." All the more reason to remember,

Whatsoever ye do, do all to the glory of God" (1 Corinthians 10:31)

10.22.02

Montgomery County, Md. — A bullet fired by an unseen gunman killed a Montgomery County bus driver shortly before dawn [Tuesday] as he stood in the lighted doorway of his empty bus, while police renewed their fitful, anxious effort to communicate with a murderous sniper who has eluded a manhunt for three weeks. If yester-day's shooting is linked to the Washington area sniper by ballistics tests, the slaying of Conrad E. Johnson, 35, which occurred in Aspen Hill, would be the 10th killing and 13th shooting attributed to the gunman ...

The final shooting took place approximately one mile from the first. Twenty days after firing into the front window of a Michaels Arts and Crafts store in Aspen Hill, Maryland, the gunmen claimed his thirteenth victim and tenth fatality.

A minute more and Conrad E. Johnson, 35, was due to start his morning run as a Montgomery County bus driver. In the pre-dawn darkness his Bus 5705 was parked at the 14100 block of Grand Pre Road in Aspen Hill, just off Connecticut Avenue. Beside the Ride On bus was a neighborhood basketball court and wooded Northgate Park. At 5:56 a.m., Tuesday, October 22, Johnson climbed to the top step of his bus and stood in the doorway, clearly framed by the cabin lights inside the vehicle. A shot rang out—for the first time in Montgomery County since the initial wave of shootings—and Johnson was hit in the rib cage. Still alive, he was rushed to Suburban Hospital in nearby Bethesda but later succumbed to his wounds. A union man and ten-year veteran of the county bus service, Johnson was the son of Jamaican immigrants and himself the father of two boys.

Ironically, the Montgomery County bus system had recently installed, on a trial basis, security cameras on ten percent of its vehicles. Bus 5705 was not one of them.

The tragic slaying punctuated a strange three-day chain of events that began with the Saturday night attack in Ashland, Virginia. There the sniper left a three-page ransom demand with instructions for making contact. Efforts to establish the contact failed, however, leaving Montgomery County Police Chief Charles Moose to attempt communicating with the killer through the media. Three times over Sunday and Monday the task force leader addressed the sniper on national television, seemingly without result.

Then the gunman gave his answer. At the scene of the October 22 slaying, police found a second letter from the sniper. The neatly handwritten note repeated the threat, made in the first letter, that "your children are not safe anywhere at any time." And once more, despite a fifth "traffic lockdown" that closed major roadways for hours, the shooter made good his escape.

That afternoon at a 4:40 press conference, Moose addressed himself to the sniper. "We have received a communication," he acknowledged. "We will be responding soon." He also acknowledged to reporters, "We remain concerned about the safety of all people in our region. We realize that the person or the people involved in this have shown a clear willingness and ability to kill people of all ages, all races, all genders, all professions, different times, different days in different locations."

Then at 7:15 p.m. he delivered another public message to the killer.

In the past several days you have attempted to communicate with us. We have researched the option [for paying ransom] you stated and found that it is not possible electronically to comply in the manner you requested. However, we remain open and ready to talk to you about the options you have mentioned. It is important that we do this without anyone else getting hurt. Call us at the same number you used before to obtain the 800 number you have requested. If you would feel more comfortable, a private P.O. box number or another secure method can be provided. You indicated that this is about more than violence. We are waiting to hear from you.

As Chief Moose spoke these words, however, he knew that the case was beginning to break open. And it all came down to three phone calls—one from Tacoma, Washington, one to a Catholic priest, and one from the sniper directly to the police.

The first break came a week earlier when, on October 17, a man claiming to be the sniper telephoned a police hotline. Angry and restive and wanting to be taken seriously, the caller told investigators to check a murder-robbery "in Montgomery" that would prove he was telling the truth. The next day, the Rev. William Sullivan, a priest at St. Ann's Roman Catholic Church in Ashland, received a call from two men. Speaking in garbled and frustrated tones, the callers used the term "I am God" and repeatedly mentioned a murder in Montgomery, Alabama.

That was Saturday. The Ashland priest did not believe he had spoken with the sniper, but only with two people who were "overly obsessed" with the case. Then that night, October 19, the sniper struck near the interstate ramp in Ashland. On Sunday morning, investigators stopped at St. Ann's Church to ask Sullivan if he might have any ideas about the shooting. He related the phone conversation that had occurred the previous day.

Sunday night, FBI agents contacted police in Montgomery, Alabama, the state capital. Did they have any unsolved killings in the city? Police Chief J.H. Wilson told investigators about a September 21 liquor store robbery in which one woman was slain and another wounded. The store was located near an interstate ramp and the killers, though chased by a rookie patrol officer, got away and were never apprehended. Found at the crime scene, however, was a guns-and-ammo magazine apparently dropped by one of the assailants.

The magazine bore a fingerprint.

FBI agents flew to Montgomery the next day, Monday, to look at the evidence. More agents arrived Tuesday as hope mounted at the sniper task force. On Wednesday, detectives from the Alabama capital flew to Washington. Using national databases not always available to local police, the FBI matched the fingerprint to an illegal immigrant with Jamaican citizenship. The teenage boy, John Lee Malvo, had been apprehended in Bellingham, Washington, and fingerprinted by the Immigration and Naturalization Service in Seattle. In a sworn statement he claimed to live with his "father," John Allen Muhammad, in a homeless shelter.

Two additional leads now drew investigators' attention to the Seattle area. First, the ATM card specified by the sniper in his Ashland ransom letter had been reported stolen on the West Coast and then used illicitly in Tacoma, Washington. Second, a resident of Tacoma had called the task force hotline to report a former neighbor who frequently did target practice with a high-powered rifle in his backyard. The man, whose name was "Muhammad," and another person nicknamed "Sniper" would fire into a tree stump.

On Wednesday morning, October 23, agents entered the duplex, removed the stump for investigation, and combed the yard with metal detectors in hopes of finding bullet fragments. Then, when authorities confirmed that Muhammad and Malvo had once lived at the Tacoma address, the trail began to get hot.

Next, investigators discovered that on September 11 Muhammad had registered a blue 1990 Chevy Caprice in the state of New Jersey. A further check turned up the fact that police in Baltimore had reported Muhammad sleeping in the Caprice on October 8—thus placing him in Maryland. Officers at the scene ran a check on his license plate but, finding the vehicle was not listed as stolen and that no warrants were outstanding for Muhammad, they let him go with a warning. Later it was learned police had run license checks on the Caprice at least ten times— the first time on October 3—due to various encounters, but could take no action. Once, the car was photographed running a red light in Fairfax, Virginia.

By Wednesday night, October 23, law enforcement authorities issued arrest warrants for Muhammad and Malvo. Then just after midnight, at 12:05 a.m., Chief Moose appeared once again on national television. He had another message for the sniper.

We understand that you communicated with us by calling several different locations. Our inability to talk has been a concern for us, as it has been for you. You have indicated that you want us to do and say certain things.

Then, at the sniper's behest, Chief Moose made a reference to a folk tale in which a boastful rabbit attempts to ensnare a duck but, as the bird flies away, the rabbit is dragged to its own death.

You have asked us to say, "We have the sniper like a duck in a noose." We understand that hearing us say this is important to you. However, we want you to know how difficult it has been to understand what you want because you have chosen to use only notes, indirect messages, and calls to other jurisdictions ...

The task force leader then urged the sniper to call a special toll-free number or write to a specified post office box, but to "be assured that we remain ready to talk with you." The making a reference to the first ransom letter found at the Ashland shooting site, Chief Moose continued.

... Our word is our bond. If we can establish communications with you, we can offer other means of addressing what you have asked for. Let's talk directly. We have an answer for you about your [ransom payment] option. We are waiting for you to contact us.

At the same press conference, Chief Moose used the media for another purpose. The task force alerted the public to a blue Chevy Caprice with New Jersey license plate NDA-21Z, warning that its occupants were "armed and dangerous" but wanted for questioning. Anyone seeing the vehicle should call 911 but take no action.

Then for the first time, shortly after midnight on October 24, the names of John Allen Muhammad and John Lee Malvo were released to the public.

Chapter Eight
The Bus Stop
and the Things We Value: Time

In another minute Conrad Johnson, 35, was due to begin his morning run. As driver of Bus 5705, he helped convey the seventy thousand daily passengers who ride Montgomery County's fleet of two hundred forty buses. Each of his stops was carefully timed according to a published schedule. People had places to go and, as a ten-year driving veteran, Johnson took pride in getting them there on time.

Life in our cities and suburbs is that way; as we strive to keep our ever-busy schedules and somehow hold our lives together. Yet the fast pace by which we live also gives us an appreciation of what we might miss—if we do not make ourselves take time for important things, things like family, friendship, community.

Conrad Johnson knew what was important. The son of Jamaican immigrants, he knew about hard work but also saw his job as more than just a paycheck. A loyal union man, he was loved by his co-workers who openly wept as news of the shooting spread over the bus system's radio dispatch service. Bus operators from as far away as Indiana drove their forty-foot coaches to Johnson's funeral at Glendale Baptist Church in Landover, Maryland. They arrived at the service in a convoy that represented some fourteen bus systems. At the memorial, the father of sons aged seven and fifteen was remembered as a man who "loved to work on cars, cook chicken curry and play football with neighborhood kids." A fitting tribute.

Time to Remember

All of us have loved ones and friends who now live far from us or who have passed away. How much we wish that we could spend more time with them! They have enriched our lives.

The more than two hundred people who jammed Ashton United Methodist Church celebrated **James Martin** as, in his pastor's words, an "American hero" and "just plain old Jim." He died while picking up sodas and snacks for his son's church youth group, one of the countless mundane chores a father does for the family he loves.

Sonny Buchanan had just gotten out of the landscaping business and moved to a new home in Virginia. But each week he made the long drive to White Flint, Maryland, to cut the grass of an old customer who needed the favor. He was pushing a Lawn-Boy mower at 7:41 in the morning when the sniper cut him down. At his memorial service, Buchanan was remembered as a landscaper and amateur poet who mentored troubled youth at the local Boys and Girls Club. Engaged to be married, he was restoring an old farmhouse in the Virginia moutains where he hoped to start a tree nursery.

Premkumar Walekar immigrated to the United States from India when he was eighteen. A cab driver and father of two, he worked hard for the day in May 2003 when his eldest child would become the first family member to earn a college degree. His daughter Andrea, a business management major at the University of Maryland, said her graduation is now "going to be a really sad day." Her father was shot and killed while refueling his cab at a gas station. "Every time I hear the garage door open, I think my father's coming home," Andrea said. His widow Margaret, however, was too saddened by the empty rooms to stay home and mourn. She returned to her work as a nurse at Montgomery General Hospital.

Sarah Ramos and **Lori Lewis Rivera** were both young mothers who each left behind a husband and small child.

Pascal Charlot, the sniper's oldest victim, was a carpenter who immigrated from Haiti in 1964 and earned his living as a home remodeler. Over the years, he raised five children who are now grown and have productive lives of their own. Charlot was retired and the sole caregiver for his wife Doriel, an Alzheimer's sufferer. The one thousand people who came to his funeral mass at Shrine of the Sacred Heart in Northwest Washington recalled Charlot's ready smile and enjoyment of wholesome pranks and his deep love for his wife. A month earlier he had taken his ailing wife out to dinner for her seventy-eighth birthday and had given her a bouquet of red roses.

Dean Harold Meyers died after working late for the engineering company he faithfully served for twenty years. Thirty years before his death Meyers had fought as an Army master sergeant in Vietnam, nearly losing the use of an arm and being decorated for his service. He had to give up playing the piano but, through vigorous rehabilitation of his arm, could resume his passion for outdoor sports. Meyers was remembered at his memorial as a "solid, conscientious" man and "loving uncle" for his many nieces and nephews. "He always remembered everyone's birthday," it was said.

On the day of his funeral, Meyers was supposed to be on the Appalachian Trail, hiking and camping with friends. Instead, the funeral program included an essay he wrote in 1972 after returning from Vietnam: "The American Dream has not soured over the years. Perhaps, we have a distorted view of our past history, believing that at one time our nation was virtuous and now is corrupt. ... How can we forget we were once a nation under the siege of civil war ... [and] once we condoned the buying and selling of a human life? Where was the American dream during those dark years? No, we have not fallen, but rather are rising."

Kenneth Bridges, father of six, was shot while passing through the Washington area on a business trip. He was well known and respected in Philadelphia as a leader in the African-American business community, a charismatic entrepreneur who founded a national distribution network for black-owned manufacturers. Bridges strongly believed in self-reliance and that African-Americans should create their own opportunities. Yet neighbors described him as the kind of man who would welcome newcomers with a basket of homemade chocolate cupcakes.

Linda Franklin, an FBI cybercrime analyst, had in the past year endured a double mastectomy and the death of a teenage niece whom she had helped raise. But she "lived life with spirit, flair and humor," according to the more than three hundred fifty family and friends who crowded her memorial service at Mount Olivet United Methodist Church in Arlington, Virginia. Having gotten her college degree at age thirty-one, she had been a teacher in Japan and Belgium, but had recently embarked on a new career with the FBI. A mother of two grown children who looked forward to becoming a grandmother, Franklin, also enjoyed hiking, river rafting, and skiing. And she was excited about moving with her husband Ted—and her two dogs and two cats—into a new home; they had been buying housewarming items when she was shot in the parking lot of a Home Depot. The movers were due to come at the end of the week. "Just a fun-loving, very friendly, loving, caring, giving person," said a friend. "It's a real loss."

A Time for Everything

These were all people who were worth spending time getting to know. Now, tragically, the opportunity is gone. Yet every day there are missed opportunities over which we do have control. Time goes by quickly as children grow up, friends move away, loved ones leave us. The words of Solomon are well known but worth repeating.

> *To every thing there is a season, and a time to every purpose under the heaven: a time to be born, and a time to die; a time to plant, and a time to pluck up that which is planted; a time to kill, and a time to heal; a time to break down, and a time to build up; a time to weep, and a time to laugh; a time to mourn, and a time to dance; a time to cast away stones, and a time to gather stones together; a time to embrace, and a time to refrain from embracing; a time to get, and a time to lose; a time to keep, and a time to cast away; a time to rend, and a time to sew; a time to keep silence, and a time to speak; a time to love, and a time to hate; a time of war, and a time of peace. (Ecclesiastes 3:1-8)*

Next, however, Solomon asks a question that is very relevant to our hectic lives today, "What profit hath he that worketh in that wherein he laboureth? I have seen the travail, which God hath given to the sons of men to be exercised in it" (3:9-10). In other words, What good is all our toil and our busyness? Solomon provides an answer when he writes,

> *He hath made every thing beautiful in his time: also he hath set the world in their heart, so that no man can find out the work that God maketh from the beginning to the end. (3:11)*

And this is why, as we set our priorities and budget our time, we must give first place to spending time with God. Because God is a good God to know, a God who created everything from beginning to end—and who can therefore make everything beautiful when, according to His wisdom, the time is right. On our own "there is no good" (3:12) in our strivings. But a man can "enjoy the good of all his labour [when] it is the gift of God" (3:13).

We can count on God's gift because the things He does are lasting and require no "help" on our part. "I know that, whatsoever God doeth, it shall be for ever: nothing can be put to it, nor any thing taken from it: and God doeth it, that men should fear before him" (3:14).

If the Lord Will

But then Solomon makes a very sober observation about time. "I said in mine heart, God shall judge the righteous and the wicked: for there is a time there for every purpose and for every work" (3:17). Even more sobering is the realization, "For that which befalleth the sons of men befalleth beasts; even one thing befalleth them: as the one dieth, so dieth the other; yea, they have all one breath ... All go unto one place; all are of the dust, and all turn to dust again" (3:19-20).

In the New Testament we also read of men who, heedless of their mortality, go about their daily business.

> Go to now, ye that say, To day or tomorrow we will go into such a city, and continue there a year, and buy and sell, and get gain: Whereas ye know not what shall be on the morrow. For what is your life? It is even a vapour, that appeareth for a little time, and then vanisheth away. For that ye ought to say, If the Lord will, we shall live, and do this, or that. (James 4:13-15)

That sounds like us, like you and me! Our commutes, our activities, our shopping, our errands—going about the busyness of suburban life, but not thinking about or giving time to God. As an antidote, King David wished he could "know mine end, and the measure of my days, what it is: that I may know how frail I am. Behold, thou hast made my days as an handbreadth; and mine age is as nothing before thee: verily every man at his best state is altogether vanity" (Psalm 39:4-5). But the objective for a right view of time is not to drive us to despair, but happily to "teach us to number our days, that we may apply our hearts unto wisdom" (Psalm 90:12).

And what is that wisdom? It is summed up at the end of the passage cited above—namely the realization that "*if the Lord will*, we shall live, and do this or that." But that raises a second question, What is the Lord's will? Here God gives a precious promise to those who know Him. "For I know the thoughts that I think toward you, saith the Lord, thoughts of peace, and not of evil, to give you an expected end" (Jeremiah 29:11).

If we give our time to God (which begins by accepting the gift of His Son to be the Savior that each of us needs) then we have God's assurance, "I know my plans for you. They are good plans, to give you My best for your life." *That* is God's will for your life and mine!

Telling Time

There is a second way that learning "to number our days" can enable us to "apply our hearts unto wisdom." It comes from knowing that, not only is the time for our own existence on earth finite, but so is the time for the existence of the earth itself.

The Bible teaches that Christ is coming again. When He completed His earthly ministry nearly two thousand years ago, the promise was given that "this same Jesus, which is taken up from you into heaven, shall so come in like manner as ye have seen him go into heaven" (Acts 1:11). We may "comfort one another with these words" of His promise (1 Thessalonians 4:18) because, as Jesus said, "if I go and prepare a place for you, I will come again, and receive you unto myself; that where I am, there ye may be also" (John 14:3).

Christians should not only be comforted by this promise, but should also be challenged. First, there is the challenge for you and me to be ready for His coming.

> *And now, little children, abide in [Christ]; that, when he shall appear, we may have confidence, and not be ashamed before him at his coming ... And every man that hath this hope in him purifieth himself, even as [Christ] is pure. (1 John 2:28, 3:3)*

> *[W]hat manner of persons ought ye to be in all holy conversation and godliness, looking for and hasting unto the coming of the day of God? ... Wherefore, beloved, seeing that ye look for such things, be diligent that ye may be found of him in peace, without spot, and blameless. (2 Peter 3:11-14)*

Second, however, is the challenge to alert others so that they might be ready for His coming, Jesus himself set the example. "I must work the works of him that sent me, while it is day: the night cometh, when no man can work" (John 9:4). Though many will scoff and say Jesus is not coming again, "The Lord is not slack concerning his promise, as some men count slackness; but is longsuffering to usward, not willing that any should perish, but that all should come to repentance" (2Peter 3:9).

There it is! There is the reason why God has tarried, because so many people—in your neighborhood, in your suburb, in your city—have not yet heard the Good News. And our response?

> *Go ye therefore, and teach all nations, baptizing them in the name of the Father, and of the Son, and of the Holy Ghost: teaching them to*

observe all things whatsoever I have commanded you: and, lo, I am
with you alway, even unto the end of the world" (Matthew 28:19).

Until the world ends, Christ is always with me. Yes, my time is valuable—and in the most important way possible. My time is valuable when I give it to Christ. It is valuable during the long commutes, the shopping trips, the things I do every day. It is valuable when I let Christ use my time, when my daily activities are not for myself, but when I go into the everyday places He would send me.

10.24.02

Frederick County, Md. — A Persian Gulf war veteran and a teenager arrested before dawn today at a Maryland rest stop are behind the deadly Washington-area sniper shootings that threw the region into panic for weeks, and ballistics tests showed that the gun found in their car fired nearly all of the shots in the violent spree, law enforcement officials said today ... The two suspects — identified as John Allen Muhammad, 41, once known as John Allen Williams, and Lee Malvo, 17 — were arrested after a flurry of police activity ... The [rest] stop is on Interstate 70 in Frederick County ...

At 12:05 a.m., Thursday, October 24, Montgomery County Police Chief Charles Moose went before the national media to deliver a message for the D.C. Sniper. He urged the killer to contact authorities directly regarding his ransom demands and to meanwhile commit no further bloodshed. After the brief statement he took no questions.

Soon, however, television and radio sets across the country were flashing the news that investigators wanted to question two men, John Allen Muhammad—also known as John Allen Williams—and John Lee Malvo. And they were looking for a blue 1990 Chevy Caprice with New Jersey license plate NDA-21Z.

One man who heard the bulletin was Ron Lantz, a truck driver doing an overnight haul on Interstate 70. He had pulled into a rest area about sixty miles northwest of Washington near the small Catoctin Mountain town of Meyersville, Maryland. There he spotted a car matching the police description of the Chevy Caprice.

An evangelical Christian, Lantz had been discussing the sniper case a week earlier with fellow truckers over his CB radio.

Spontaneously, he and other drivers urged all truckers within CB range to pull off the road for a prayer meeting. At least fifty truckers and a large number of other motorists participated, asking God for the capture of the sniper. As it turned out, the prayer meeting took place just twenty miles from the Meyersville rest stop.

When Lantz saw the Caprice, he quickly called 911 to alert the authorities. Then he persuaded another driver to join him as one truck blocked the rest stop entrance and the other closed the exit. Asked later by reporters about the danger to himself, Lantz responded, "My wife asked me what I would've done if they had shot me. I replied, 'I do not know, but I'm going to heaven, anyway.'"

The Capture

The 911 call was placed by Lantz at 12:47 a.m. By 1 a.m. a dozen or more Maryland state troopers set up a perimeter, roadblocked the rest stop entrance and exit, and stopped all traffic on I-70. The Caprice was parked by itself, not adjacent to any other vehicles, but it was not immediately apparent whether the car was occupied. Troopers maintained their cordon but did not approach, following instructions to first notify the sniper task force.

Within minutes a helicopter was dispatched, landing on a high school field near the task force headquarters in Montgomery County, Maryland. A squad of county officers and FBI agents, dressed in black SWAT gear, boarded the helicopter and took off northwest to the city of Frederick some ten miles from the Meyersville rest stop. Once in place, about 3:30 a.m. the team rushed the Caprice, shattered two of its windows, and captured Muhammad and Malvo without resistance. The two suspects were sleeping in the car, apparently unaware their names and likenesses were being broadcast nationwide.

Inside the vehicle police found a rifle tripod, silencer, and a Bushmaster XM-15 high-powered rifle. The weapon was quickly conveyed to the Bureau of Alcohol, Tobacco, and Firearms laboratory in Rockville, Maryland, and positively identified as the gun which fired the bullets in eleven of the fourteen Washington area shootings. In the other three attacks, bullet fragments were too badly damaged for analysis. Investigators also discovered the Caprice had been modified so that a person lying in the trunk could fire through a hole cut in the rear—though they did not know if the snipers had actually used this method.

Thought investigators could not immediately unravel the operational details of the shootings, information about the suspects themselves soon emerged in news reports.

The Suspects

John Allen Muhammad was born in New Orleans as John Allen Williams on December 31, 1960, and grew up in Baton Rouge, Louisiana. Upon graduation from high school, in 1978 he enlisted in the Louisiana Army National Guard and served six months on active duty. In 1982 he was twice court-martialed, once for failure to report for duty and obey a lawful command, and once for striking an officer. After seven years in the Guard, Muhammad was discharged in 1985 and that same year reenlisted in the regular Army.

By then Muhammad had a wife, Carol, whom he married in 1981, and a son born in 1982. About the time Muhammad joined the Army, he moved in with another woman and separated from his wife. Two years later, in 1987, the estranged couple divorced. Custody of their child was disputed and, when Muhammad was posted to Fort Lewis in Washington state, he complained that his ex-wife permitted few visits with their son.

Muhammad remarried in 1988, to a Baton Rouge woman he had dated since 1985, and in time the couple had three children. Living in Tacoma, he earned extra money by operating an auto repair service out of his home. In 1991 he was called overseas and served in the Persian Gulf War. He returned, according to his wife Mildred, "a changed man" who was bitter, angry, and controlling. In 1994 he retired from the Army with the rank of sergeant and concentrated on his auto repair service. Neighbors described a "model family," but in reality the Muhammads' marriage was deteriorating.

By 1996, in a custody proceeding over Muhammad's son by his first marriage, his second wife felt compelled to side with the mother. From then on—though Muhammad and his wife both converted to Islam in 1997—relations between the couple were increasingly strained. The pressure mounted when the auto business started to founder. Muhammad and a partner tried to start a karate school but could not attract enough students. When the school closed, the two men feuded bitterly over their debts.

SHOTS IN THE DARK

In September 1999 Muhammad moved out of the house and three months later his wife filed for divorce.

A turning point came in March 2000 when Muhammad picked up his three children from school, promising his ex-wife to return them by five, but he never showed up. He called to say they were shopping, but in reality Muhammad and the children were at the airport with tickets for the Caribbean island of Antigua. Muhammad and the children entered that country under false names and with faked documents.

Antigua was apparently chosen because one of Muhammad's auto repair customers in Tacoma had a cousin who lived in the island nation. The customer arranged for Muhammad and his children to stay for free at the cousin's home, thinking the family was going on a vacation. Once in Antigua, however, Muhammad obtained citizenship by altering his birth certificate, pasting in as his "mother" the name of a local Antiguan woman. Yet he was unable to produce paperwork needed to get a job, and so he resorted to repairing cars and selling fraudulent documents to islanders desiring to immigrate to the United States.

One of these documents was sold to Una James, a Jamaican who had immigrated illegally to Antigua in 1998 or 1999 with her son Lee Malvo—who had been born in 1985. Sometime in late 2000, James announced she would visit Jamaica to see her ailing mother. Malvo was left behind and, after several weeks when James failed to return, the boy was forced to give up his lodgings. It is believed that Muhammad may have helped James leave the island to find work in the U.S.

By this time Muhammad had been evicted from his "vacation" home when the owner learned he had kidnaped his children. He moved into a house shared by a number of people, who hung sheets from the living room ceiling to separate their living space. It was here that Malvo, in December 2000 or January 2001, moved in with Muhammad. In the absence of the boy's mother, a bond was formed. The teenager started showing a great interest in Islam. And he began using his guardian's first name as his own, becoming known as John Lee Malvo.

The Return

In March 2001, a year after arriving in Antigua, Muhammad was caught at the local airport with faked documents; he was detained but slipped away. This may have prompted him to leave

Antigua. By April 2001 Muhammad and his children, now joined by Malvo, had reentered the United States using false documents. That month, records of the Tacoma Municipal Court show that Muhammad legally changed his name from Williams to John Allen Muhammad.

He moved to Bellingham, Washington—near the Canadian border, about one hundred miles north of Tacoma—and in August 2001 enrolled his three natural children in school under false names. They were soon discovered, however. Muhammad had, meanwhile, called twice and threatened to kill his ex-wife, according to her testimony. She described him to authorities as having been a "demolition/weapons expert" in the Army who could "make a weapon out of anything."

The courts granted her a restraining order against Muhammad and, in August 2001, directed the sheriff's office in Bellingham to take the couple's three children; subsequently, the court awarded her custody. The court also ruled that Muhammad had demonstrated "abusive use of conflict" and could have an adverse impact on his children's lives, thus terminating his visitation rights.

The children told sheriff's deputies they had an "older brother" but did not give his name. That "brother," John Lee Malvo, however, rejoined his mother who was working at a Red Lobster restaurant in Fort Myers, Florida. Records show that for thirty-nine days Malvo attended a local high school there.

By October 2001, however, Muhammad and Malvo and Una James were together in Bellingham. That month, the two men began living together as "father and son" at the Lighthouse Mission, a homeless shelter in the city. James took up residence at the Agape Women's Shelter. Their lives settled into a semblance of normality as Muhammad and Malvo took out a family membership at the nearby YMCA, using the weight room and playing basketball together. Malvo even enrolled at the Bellingham high school.

Within two months, it all started to unravel. School officials became suspicious when promised transcripts and paperwork for Malvo never arrived. Concerned that the teen might be a runaway or living with someone not really his father, the school alerted police who interviewed Malvo on December 18, 2001. The following day, police were called to a "domestic disturbance" between James and Muhammad. Again police were led to Malvo, who was detained with his mother by immigration officials. The pair were released pending a hearing scheduled for November 2002, the closest available date.

The Journey

At this point, the activities of Muhammad and Malvo become murky. For a time, the pair lived in a Tacoma duplex where they disturbed neighbors by turning their backyard into a rifle range. As for the Bushmaster rifle itself, Muhammad somehow obtained it illegally; the restraining order against him barred Muhammad from owning firearms.

However, a chain of events was now forming that would eventually lead to the Nation's Capital.

When Mildred Muhammad gained custody of her three children, the court also granted permission to relocate outside Washington state without telling her husband the destination. In late 2001, she moved into a townhouse in Prince George's County, Maryland, a suburb of Washington, D.C. Somehow, John Allen Muhammad apparently learned her whereabouts. Thus began a cross-country trip that would end in a crime spree unprecedented in American history.

On February 12, 2002, Muhammad was arrested for shoplifting twenty-seven dollars in groceries from a convenience store in Tacoma. Authorities now suspect he may have returned on February 16 to Tacoma and gunned down Keenya Cook, 21, whose family had helped his ex-wife. The woman's aunt had once been a bookkeeper for Muhammad's auto repair service. Cook was staying with her aunt that day and, when she answered someone at the front door, she was shot once in the face.

Muhammad and Malvo are known to have traveled by bus from Los Angeles to Tucson, Arizona, on March 13. The pair was greeted by Muhammad's sister who lived on a nearby Air Force base. Police now suspect that Muhammad and Malvo may have been responsible for the unsolved sniper-style shooting of a man who was playing golf on a course less than two miles from the base. Jerry Ray Taylor, 60, was golfing alone about 2:15 p.m. in a practice area of the Tucson course when he was apparently shot and killed by rifle fire.

Court papers in the federal gun charge against Muhammad place him in Tacoma in the summer of 2002. A former roommate who came to visit then, later testified that Muhammad showed him an AR-15 assault rifle with a scope. He kept the weapon in an aluminum case and fantasized, "Can you imagine the damage you could do if you could shoot with a silencer?" Muhammad and "an associate" had a book on how to make a silencer and also said they were taking the weapon to a rifle range to align the scope and ensure accurate shooting.

By September 5, 2002, Muhammad and Malvo were on the East Coast. On that date a laptop computer was stolen from a pizzeria in Prince George's County; it was found in the Muhammad's Chevy Caprice when he was captured. Three thousand dollars were also taken, and the employee who was closing the restaurant was shot six times. The man later recovered from his wounds. The pizzeria was located about a mile from the Clinton, Maryland, townhouse where Mildred Muhammad and her children were living.

Three days after the pizzeria shooting, Muhammad was in Trenton, New Jersey, looking for a used car at Sure Shot Auto Sales. He settled on a blue 1990 Chevy Caprice with 146,975 miles. The two hundred fifty dollars needed for the purchase were loaned to him by Nathaniel Osbourne, the New Jersey brother of someone Muhammad knew in Antigua. Osbourne told investigators that Muhammad and Malvo apparently arrived by bus after traveling across the country. They wanted a car to continue their travels, and Osbourne, out of pity, befriended the penniless pair and loaned them the money. He was likely the last person to have regular contact with the killers.

Muhammad purchased the Caprice on September 10 using a Maryland drivers license and Maryland insurance, according to the salesman. At first Muhammad said he was buying the car for his "son," then changed his story and claimed the vehicle would be used as a cab. Then he asked the salesman if the Caprice had a spare tire and jack since he was planning a trip to Washington. On September 11, Muhammad registered the car and received New Jersey license plate NDA-21Z.

From evidence gathered by investigators, it is believed Muhammad and Malvo may have returned to Maryland and committed successive robberies of Washington suburban liquor stores on September 14 and 15. Both crimes were committed late at night and in both incidents the store clerk was wounded but recovered.

The two shooters then, police believe, may have gone on a deadly road trip to Muhammad's hometown of Baton Rouge. Muhammad and Malvo are suspected in the killing of Million [sic] Woldemariam on September 21 in Atlanta; of robbing a liquor store that same day in Montgomery, Alabama, shooting two women and killing one; and in the September 23 shooting death of Hong Im Ballenger in front of a Baton Rouge beauty salon.

Nine days later, October 2, 5:20 p.m., a bullet crashed through the front window of the Michaels Arts and Crafts store in Aspen Hill, Maryland. At 6:04 p.m., James D. Martin was gunned down in the parking lot of the Shoppers Food Warehouse in Wheaton. Over the next twenty days, another twelve attacks would leave nine more dead and three wounded.

If all the shootings under investigation—Tacoma, Tucson, Atlanta, Montgomery, Baton Rouge, Maryland, the District of Columbia, Virginia—were committed by the same men, the toll would be fifteen dead and seven wounded. Twenty-two in a dozen police jurisdictions. And with the many unsolved murders and crimes that happen daily in America, the exact count may never be known.

The Reason

Why did John Allen Muhammad and John Lee Malvo kill on such a scale? That too may never be completely known. Muhammad was an angry, frustrated, violent man who raged over custody battles with two former wives. Malvo was an unloved boy who sought a father figure.

Though Muhammad is known to have expressed satisfaction over the 9/11 bombings in New York and Washington, authorities do not believe he was connected to any terrorist organization. His targeting of the Nation's Capital apparently was dictated by the discovery of his second wife and their three children living in the suburbs of Maryland.

In a four-hour interview with *The Washington Post*, Mildred Muhammad speculated on what moved her former husband to kill. "I'm sure he had me in his scope," she said. "This [sniping] was an elaborate plan to make this look like I was a victim so he could come in as the grieving father and take the children." By perpetrating a series of seemingly random sniper shootings, Muhammad may have believed he could gun down his ex-wife without casting suspicion on himself and also obtain custody of his children.

"They all died," Mildred Muhammad said of the sniper's victims, "because of me."

Looking back, she also sees a possible connection to Michaels Arts and Crafts. The national chain was, according to the *Post* report, "one of her favorite stores when she and her husband were living in Tacoma, Washington. It was at a Michaels that she had purchased the materials she needed to fashion a bride and groom to put atop their wedding cake."

Home Depot was another frequent shopping destination for the couple in Tacoma. And if her ex-husband knew the stores she liked best then, according to Mildred Muhammad's speculation, he could shoot her without creating any suspicion of a personal connection. She also noted the warning given by the sniper in his two letters, "Your children are not safe anywhere at any time." That message, she believed, was meant for her.

Ironically, Mildred Muhammad said, her husband has achieved some of his aim. Given the national notoriety of the case, she explained, "The one thing that I came out here [to Maryland] to do I still can not do. Because now that he's been caught, I can not go out and I can not do those things that are necessary for us to live a normal life. So he is still in control."

A Postscript

In news reports of Malvo's initial testimony to police, the seventeen-year-old youth admitted being the gunman in four of the sniper attacks. He claimed responsibility for the shootings of Pascal Charlot, Linda Franklin, Conrad Johnson, and the thirteen-year-old boy who was wounded in front of his Maryland middle school.

The day after Malvo's testimony, the middle schooler was released from Washington Children's Hospital and went home to his parents. By then, the two other victims who survived the attacks in Spotsylvania and Ashland were also out of danger.

Though the sniper task force was headquartered in Montgomery County, and eight of the fourteen shootings occurred in Maryland, the two suspects were initially detained by federal authorities under a federal anti-extortion law. U.S. Attorney General John Ashcroftthen handed over the two suspects to Virginia authorities for trial, believing the crimes should be tried first where the maximum sentencing options were available.

By this he meant that Maryland, though it has capital punishment on the books, currently has a moratorium on the penalty. Neither does the state allow the death penalty for juveniles such as the seventeen-year-old Malvo, but only life imprisonment without parole as themost severe sentence. Some observers, however, noted that the cases with the most evidence for trying the two suspects were those in Maryland. Others expressed outrage that the Attorney General's decision would be driven by, in their view, a rush to seek the strongest penalty rather than try the strongest case.

The Commonwealth of Virginia is a steadfast practitioner of capital punishment and also permits the sanction to be imposed on juveniles. Since the U.S. Supreme Court reinstated the death penalty in 1976, the state is second only to Texas in the number of capital sentences carried out. The cases of Muhammad and Malvo may break new legal ground as the first to be tried under a new Virginia anti-terrorism statute. Under the law, enacted in the wake of 9/11, capital punishment may be imposed whether or not the suspect in a terrorist act was the one who actually pulled the trigger.

The framers of the law could have never imagined the case under which it would be tested.

Epilogue
The Rest Stop
and the Questions That Remain

Meyersville, Maryland, is set among the rolling foothills of the Catoctin Mountains. Camp David, the presidential retreat, is nearby. So is the Appalachian Trail. History buffs visit the area to see Antietam National Battlefield and, just across the West Virginia line, Harpers Ferry. Numerous state parks dot the region, while the many working farms preserve its rural character.

Driving down the main street of Meyersville, urban America seems far away. Yet Meyersville has the good fortune, say local boosters, of being located on Interstate 70 at the midpoint between the growing cities of Frederick and Hagerstown, Maryland. Washington, D.C., itself lies only sixty miles to the southeast.

And so if you continue north on main street, just outside of town you will see an old farm sprouting a new crop—of subdivisions and single-family homes. Such a home was the last home my parents bought together, the home they owned when my father died. The house was situated on a rise, and I loved the view from their back-yard patio, of the farmland on the other side of the subdivision and the mountains beyond. By now, the new section of the subdivision has opened and the view is not quite as good.

It was at the I-70 rest stop beside Meyersville that John Allen Muhammad and John Lee Malvo were arrested about 3:30 a.m. while sleeping in a blue 1990 Chevy Caprice, apparently unaware that police were looking specifically for them. A truck driver spotted the car and called 911. The two suspects were arrested without incident.

I stayed up much of the night on October 23, 2002, watching TV reports that suggested a break in the case was imminent. But midnight passed, and I went to bed. The next morning I awoke to the news of the arrests and that police had matched a gun in the suspects' car to the shootings. My first reaction was relief. My second was overwhelming astonishment. *Meyersville? They made the arrests at Meyersville! My mother and father lived there!* It was the final shock that led me to write this book.

'This Is Crazy'

John Allen Muhammad and John Lee Malvo are innocent until proven guilty. That assumption is part of our system and I have faith that, in the end, our system, will do justice. But in the days after the arrests were made, it was enough for me to know that the murder weapon was off the streets and that the shootings—fourteen in a span of twenty days, leaving ten dead and three wounded—had stopped.

But the attacks, called unprecedented by many experts, left me with many questions. During those days I canceled a business trip to Washington. The shooting sites were too familiar, too easy for my family back in South Carolina to envision, and I could not put them through the agony of worry. When two people were shot just minutes from my mother's new home in Fredericksburg, Virginia, she and I discussed our worries via e-mail. She wrote,

> *Each sniper attack happened very, very close. One just down the street and one only five minutes away. I was worried about driving back home so I changed my route ... It was fine but I had to go to the grocery store and that meant going by the Exxon [scene of the eleventh shooting]. I saw four police cars right in that area. I have to admit it was scary and there was not a soul in the grocery store. Thanks for your prayers, and tell me why this is happening? What is going on in the world now? ... This is just crazy. Everyone here stays home.*

Why is this happening? What is going in the world now? My struggle to resolve these questions—and the answers I came to—are the substance of this book. For me, writing is often the best therapy. It helped me work through these issues. And yet, several questions still linger in my mind.

Four Questions

First, can we ever return to the complacency of our suburban lives? There are many in our society who are willing to commit violence, some who harbor a perverse craving for attention and a desire to exert power by instilling fear. The D.C. Sniper has provided a shockingly effective blueprint for the next copycat killer who decides to come along.

Second, though the sniper committed an unprecedented crime, will we be anymore successful in stopping the death toll a second time around? Despite the efforts of police forces in more than half a dozen jurisdictions in a major American city—even the help of the FBI and the military—the gunmen perpetrated an incredible fourteen shootings in just twenty days. Massive police dragnets were unsuccessful. The very nature of our suburban road systems, with their quick and almost limitless alternate routes, seemingly defeated attempts to catch the killers. Only the suspects' own mistake, say news reports, led to their capture.

Third, suppose a professional, organized attempt were made to employ the tactics of the D.C. Sniper? Police conclude the gunmen acted alone under the compulsion of their twisted minds. What if a trained terrorist organization were behind such attacks? Sniping requires little in the way of cost, equipment, or logistics. Now we know it inflicts maximum terror. The thought of sniper-terrorism is truly horrifying but, after 9/11, no longer unthinkable.

Finally, the D.C. Sniper attacked places that are integral to our modern suburban lives—the shopping center, the gas station, the restaurant, the neighborhood school. One man was shot while mowing the lawn. Downtown Washington, with its narrow streets and crowded buildings, offers few vantages for a sniper. But the suburbs—with their broad avenues, spacious common areas, and plentiful trees—are a different story. As the sniper attacks mounted, I could not help but think of another suburban institution where people gather in parking lots, namely, our churches.

Religiously motivated terrorism is all too familiar in our world today. Jerusalem and Tel Aviv, for example, are modern cities not unlike Washington. Though security in Israel is far more intrusive than most Americans would tolerate, terrorists still strap bombs to their bodies and blow up public restaurants and buses. Will the faithful in America someday face the prospect of death for attending their houses of worship?

If so, how would Christians respond? How would I respond? How would you respond?

Is Jesus worth it? That is the real question. Today our American cities and suburbs afford a level of personal empowerment that is unparalleled in human history. In October 2002, the people of our nation's capital glimpsed what it would be like to lose that which we take for granted. We were shocked at the senseless loss of life and fearful of how our daily routines were restricted. We would not willingly give up our way of life, nor should we.

But if you or I were threatened for being a Christian, would we be as worried about giving up our faith? About giving up our Savior? Would we be as unwilling to give up our visits to church as we would our trips to the mall?

When we face the prospect of losing something, that is when we discover what is important to us, what we value. In American today we value our choices and autonomy, our convenience and abundance. Do we value Christ?

Acknowledgments

Few times in my career have I felt so impressed of God to write with such unavoidable urgency. But a writer cannot make a book happen by himself. Every book is a partnership between writer and publisher. I am grateful for the partnership and support of my publisher, Tomm Knutson, who immediately caught the vision for this book, marshaled the resources to make it happen, and gave me the encouragement to complete it. A book of this nature is most valuable to readers when it can reach them at their time of greatest need or interest. Without the prayers of family and friends, and especially my colleagues and students at Bob Jones University, I could not have sustained the strength and endurance to do my work in the required time. I also wish to acknowledge my hometown newspaper, *The Washington Post*, of which I have been a loyal reader for more than thirty years. It is a world-class newspaper and its website, which was an invaluable source of information for me on the sniper murders, is consistently rated the best newspaper website in America. I agree. Most of all, I am grateful for the support of my wife Donna and children Mark Jr. and Laura who have always encouraged me to follow the calling of God to write. Living with someone who is on deadline is not always easy. But they give me "space" to write when I need it, and they give me their wholehearted and unconditional love when I need that—which is all the time.

About the Author

Mark Ward Sr. is a gifted Christian communicator whom God has used as an author, broadcaster, educator, and speaker. He is author of six books including two histories of religious broadcasting, *The Music in the Air: Hymn & Song Stories from the Golden Age of Radio* and *Air of Salvation: The Story of Christian Broadcasting*, and has appeared on numerous national Christian talk shows as a commentator on religious media. A contributor to leading religious and business journals, he has been a frequent speaker at Christian writers conferences nationwide and serves on the advisory board of the American Christian Writers Association. As a broadcaster Mark has been producer and speaker for the nationally syndicated daily radio programs *The Word Works!*, stories of conversions through gospel literature that have now been published as a book, and *Home School Helper* which is currently heard on more than three hundred stations. He is a professor of radio and television broadcasting at Bob Jones University, Greenville, South Carolina, and also directs syndication of the school's radio programming on Christian stations nationwide. Mark lives with his wife Donna in Greenville, where his children Mark Jr. and Laura are students at Bob Jones University. He is available to speak at churches and conferences by contacting SendForth Media, Box 34577, Greenville, South Carolina 29614, or e-mailing *sendforth@bju.edu*.

About You

This book has asked questions about life and death. If you have been asking the same questions, you should be glad to know that Jesus has "come that they might have life, and that they might have it more abundantly" (John 10:10) and, more importantly, that "ye may *know* that ye have eternal life" (1 John 5:13).

How can you *know* that you have eternal life? Maybe you are asking, "How can I know if I have done enough good works to outweigh the bad?" But the "good news" is that salvation is not something you must earn. God wants you to have it as a *gift!* Jesus Christ has *already* paid the penalty for your sins. But a gift cannot be yours until you *receive* it from the giver. So how do you do that? The Bible says . . .

I need a Savior. "For all have sinned and come short of the glory of God" (Romans 3:23). "But your iniquities have separated between you and your God" (Isaiah 59:2).

Christ died for me. "For Christ also hath suffered for sins, the just for the unjust, that He might bring us to God" (1 Peter 3:18).

I need to repent of my sin. "He that covereth his sins shall not prosper: but whoso confesseth and forsaketh them shall have mercy" (Proverbs 28:13). "Repent ye therefore, and be converted, that your sins may be blotted out" (Acts 3:19).

I must received Jesus by faith. "But as many as received Him, to them gave He power to become the sons of God, even to them that believe on His name" (John 1:12).

I can be sure of my salvation. "He that hath the Son hath life" (1 John 5:12). "Verily, verily, I say unto you, he that heareth My word, and believeth on Him that sent Me, hath everlasting life, and shall not come into condemnation; but is passed from death unto life" (John 5:24).

If you would like to respond to what you have just read about receiving eternal life through Jesus Christ then—if you mean it—pray the following prayer or say to God in your own words what is said following:

Dear Jesus, I realize that I am a sinner and that I need a Savior. I believe You are the Holy Son of God who died on the cross to pay the penalty for my sins and bring me to God. I am sorry for my sins. By faith I receive You as my personal Savior. I receive Your free gift of eternal life which You have offered to all who believe on Your name, and now I place my trust in Your salvation. Amen.

If you have received Jesus Christ as you Savior, get a copy of God's Word—the Bible—for yourself and begin reading it every day. Start talking to God each day in prayer. And find a church where the Bible is believed and Christ is preached and go there regularly.

Let us know about your decision. If we can help you get started in your new Christian life, or if you still have not yet decided to receive Christ and have more questions, please write us at: Ambassador-Emerald International, 427 Wade Hampton Boulevard, Greenville, South Carolina 29609. You may also call (864) 235-2434 or send an e-mail through our website at *www.emeraldhouse.com.*

Other Books by Mark Ward, Sr.

The Music in the Air
Hymn & Song Stories from
the Golden Age of Radio

Radio's golden age was an exciting time of great preachers, great quartets, and great songwriters who gave us some of the world's best Christian music. Read the exciting stories of radio pioneers like Charles Fuller; groups like the Old-Fashioned Revival Hour Quartet, the Blackwood Brothers and The Statesmen; and songwriters like John W. Peterson, Mosie Lister, Ira Stanphill, and Stuart Hamblen.

The Word Works!
151 Amazing Stories of Men and Women
Saved Through Gospel Literature

Ever give out a gospel tract and wonder if it did any good? Now you can find out! How? Through this amazing collection of 151 true stories of men and women around the world who were saved by picking up or receiving gospel literature in miraculous ways.

Coming Soon!
Authentic Worship
Traditional, Contemporary, Biblical:
What Do the Scriptures Say?

Written with Dr. David Whitcomb, this important new books goes beyond the rhetoric on both sides to see what actual examples of worship in the Bible—from Genesis to Revelation—teach us about worship that pleases God.

Ask for them at your local bookstore or contact:
Ambassador-Emerald International
1-800-209-8570 • www.emeraldhouse.com